Holy Clarity

Holy Clarity

~

The Practice of Planning and Evaluation

Sarah B. Drummond

THE
ALBAN
INSTITUTE
Herndon, Virginia
www.alban.org

The Alban Institute
2121 Cooperative Way, Suite 100
Herndon, VA 20171

Unless otherwise noted, all Scripture quotations are from the New Revised Standard Version of the Bible, copyright © 1989, Division of Christian Education of the National Council of the Churches of Christ in the United States of America, and are used by permission.

Cover design by Spark Design.

Author's photo by Len Rubenstein (www.lenrubenstein.com).

Library of Congress Cataloging-in-Publication Data

Drummond, Sarah B.
  Holy clarity : the practice of planning and evaluation / Sarah B. Drummond.
      p. cm.
  Includes bibliographical references.
  ISBN 978-1-56699-387-6
  1. Christian leadership. 2. Church management. I. Title.

  BV652.1.D745 2009
  253—dc22
                            2009012568

09   10   11   12   13   VP   5   4   3   2   1

For my husband Dan

Contents

∼

Foreword

~

In St. Louis, Missouri, there was a church with a wonderfully simple name—Jesus Church. A German immigrant congregation, Jesus Church served its surrounding community faithfully for over a hundred years. For nearly seventy years of its life, Jesus Church was served by the same pastor. That this pastor might serve forever was a joke in some circles. Of course, he did not: no pastor serves forever.

Every pastor has a first day, when she or he begins serving a congregation, and a last day of service to the congregation. Between these two days much happens: sermons are preached; baptisms, weddings, and funerals are performed; pastoral calls are made; and prayers are prayed. Although much happens, it is remarkable how rarely what happens is self-conscious, intentional, or reflective. Far too often, pastors and the congregations they lead do not think carefully or intentionally about what will happen between these two days. There is little explicit planning and nearly no conscious evaluation. What they are doing, why they are doing it, and what difference any of it makes remain unclear. Although unclear, the things these pastors and the congregations they serve are doing can and do matter; they make a difference. It is Professor Sarah Drummond's argument in this book that getting clear about what is being done, why it is being done, and how it is being done can help a religious community make the kind of difference it ought to make.

Religious communities ought to make a difference. If all is fine in the world—if there are no problems, no worries—then religious organizations can blissfully live without clarity about the difference they make. But it is patently untrue that all is well with the world. There is far too much at stake for congregations and their leaders to fail to take stock of what they are doing and how well they are doing it.

Fortunately, a new generation of scholarship has begun to give counsel on church leadership. This new scholarship, interdisciplinary in its approach, is boldly making the important point that it is high time religious leaders start to lead. A body of literature is taking shape, lectures are being given, seminary curricula are being revised—leadership as an issue in the church is appearing on the radar screen. Let us hope it is not too late.

This book is an important contribution to this new body of church leadership literature. Sarah Drummond is a fine scholar. Drawing from fields as diverse as business management and biblical studies, her interdisciplinary method gives lead to a new approach to church life. She observes that "ministry programs function for years without ministry leaders' expressing the condition that led to their creation and that justifies their continuation." Such muddling along without evaluation or planning has contributed to the decline, wastefulness, and lethargy of too many congregations. As Dr. Drummond is aware, evaluation and planning are sometimes threatening to leaders. However, she is a seasoned coach of program evaluators and in this book she provides a good mix of practical wisdom and encouragement.

Leadership may mean many different things in different settings, but it surely means having a vision for the future and taking deliberate, thoughtful, and faithful steps toward it. Leadership involves change. Change is not something a leader brings to a congregation; it is already there. The question, of course, is not whether one changes but how one changes and toward what end. There is no doubt that churches are usually slow to change. As Dr. Drummond notes, churches are frequently "governed by standing committees that move methodically and slowly, even when significant issues (such as rapid membership decline) arise." It may not be bad that churches are slow to change—after all, they are carriers of ancient traditions and practices. But it is surely bad if they are not clear about how they respond to the changes in the circumstances that envelop them. Good and faithful leaders are needed in congregations to help them make faithful steps in changing conditions.

In 1999, the congregation called Jesus Church closed its doors for the last time. The neighborhood it served had profoundly changed, and its membership had fallen to a faithful few. The last members of the congregation distributed the church's remaining resources among a few ministries and organizations it had supported over its life.

The closing of a congregation called Jesus Church does not portend the closing of the church of Jesus Christ. When a congregation has completed a season of ministry, it is surely fitting for it to come to a graceful end. There is no disgrace in ending, when the time is right. This is where good leadership is needed. Good leadership helps discern the times: Is it time to stop doing what once seemed the right thing to do? Or is it time to keep on keeping on? When do you know what to do, how to do it, and exactly when to begin doing it?

How can one be clear? Such holy clarity is never easy to obtain. But as this book wisely argues, such holy clarity is to be treasured, pursued vigorously, and celebrated joyously when it breaks forth. Knowing what moment we are in is very important for leadership. For the church in the United States, this is a significant moment. There are many signs of flagging vitality and shifting paradigms. A moment in the United States is not the same as a moment for the church throughout the world. In very many places around the world, the church of Jesus Christ is thriving and flourishing. Our place in global Christianity is among the most important matters about which United States pastors and leaders of congregations need to gain clarity.

I have little doubt that God has hopes and plans for the church in the United States. I have serious doubts that the hopes and plans for the church in the United States are the same as they were even a generation ago. In order to discern what God is calling our churches to be and do now, we should fervently pray for "holy clarity."

David M. Greenhaw
President
Eden Theological Seminary

Preface

~

LEADERSHIP AND EVALUATION ARE NOT SEPARATE disciplines. Evaluative activities are part of the work of a leader, and some of the best practices of evaluation mirror the qualities that make a leader effective. Here are just a few examples:

- Leaders understand that without a goal or vision, they will not be able to motivate a community to move forward. Similarly, evaluators understand that their practice relies upon commonly understood benchmarks. Evaluation is meaningless without something against which to evaluate. As evaluation scholars Marcia Festen and Marianne Philbin put it, "Before you can evaluate, you need to decide what you're looking for. For every program, initiative, or aspect of your mission you want to explore and evaluate, therefore, you need to have a clear goal statement to consult."[1]
- Leaders understand that it is not any one person's job to define the goals of an organization, but rather that of stakeholders who must work together to shape a vision. Evaluators know that goals or benchmarks are best developed collaboratively, with numerous stakeholders working together to describe success before any evaluation takes place.
- When conducting an evaluation using survey data, good evaluators know better than to lump into general findings the one or two surveys that vary radically from the sample as a whole. They understand that data coming from "outliers" need to be treated with care. Sometimes, if the sample is

large, those surveys are excluded from overall calculations. If the sample is smaller, evaluators know that they will have to provide an explanation for the outliers and how they might have skewed the results. In a similar way, good leaders know that they must pay attention to the one or two voices of dissent or difference among those in the communities they lead. But they cannot allow those voices to steer the community off course; rather, they need to take dissent into account without allowing it to dominate the conversation.

- Good leaders know that they must focus their efforts on bringing about transformation in the communities they serve. They give more energy to serving those communities than they do to pursuing their own interests, and they base their choice of activities on what they think the community needs most from them. In an analogous way, evaluation calls upon leaders to look at the effectiveness of the organization's work from an "outcomes perspective." An experienced evaluator spends less time posing "process questions," such as "Did you enjoy the worship service?" and more time on questions about outcomes, such as "How is your faith changing since you began attending this church?"

Leaders need to know what is happening in their organizations and how those activities are effecting change. Evaluation exists to serve that need, and its best practices are shaped by a desire to learn. Yet even given the symbiotic relationship between leadership and evaluation, leaders commonly resist evaluation. In part, this reluctance relates to our national culture of busyness and the overwhelming nature of leadership in complex organizations. If a leader sees evaluation as something separate from his or her daily work,[2] as just one more task on an overflowing list, setting it aside is understandable. But I fear that there is a deeper reason why evaluation, and its integral role in leadership, causes anxiety.

I met recently with a denominational leader who works with pastors. In discussing a new pastor's difficulties in her first call, he told me that the church had conducted an all-church evaluation and that the pastor had been devastated by the results. It took me a few moments to realize that he meant that the church evaluated *the pastor*, because when he said "all-church evaluation," I had jumped to the conclusion that the church's entire program, including all of its leaders, had been reviewed through a comprehensive process.

Instead, I learned, the church used a survey that broadly laid out the kinds of work the survey writers thought ministers ought to do, with no regard for the congregation's specific expectations of the pastor, as laid out in her call agreement. The pastor received mostly positive feedback, but negative "outliers" were lumped in with the rest of the survey data. The way the data were presented to her made it hard for her to understand whether one person was upset with her performance on many levels, or several were disappointed in limited ways. I, of course, could understand why she felt hurt, and I attribute much of the injury to a poorly executed evaluation. This process skipped some of the most basic tasks of evaluation (collaborative discussion on the nature of "success," clear and measurable goals, careful treatment of outliers). Furthermore, it was not designed in such a way that the pastor could learn, with learning as a primary goal. It is likely that some angry congregants wished to use evaluation as a way to prove a point. It is also quite possible that well-meaning parishioners interpreted language in the church bylaws about evaluation to mean that an evaluation is necessarily closed-ended and adversarial, rather than participatory and appreciative.

I am tempted to say that this book seeks to bring evaluation "back to basics," but to suggest a bringing back would indicate that there ever *was* a better time for evaluation in religious organizations. In fact, evaluation is a relatively new concept for most churches and even for most nonprofit organizations. When the "bottom line" of an organization does not take the form of dollars and cents, evaluation is a complex undertaking and one that is only beginning to be appreciated as a necessary leadership task. In this book, however, I will look at the most basic reason why we evaluate: to find and to create clarity in our religious organization's sense of purpose, and to see the truth when we investigate the impact of our activities. I believe that clarity is holy and pleasing to God and that any leadership practice that brings greater clarity into institutions that seek to follow God's will is an inherently useful practice.

This book will explore holy clarity and the way evaluation can help us find it.

In chapter 1, I describe how our postmodern cultural context makes clarity harder to attain than it used to be, and why evaluation has emerged (not without complications) as a response to that cultural reality.

In chapter 2, I look at holy clarity from a biblical and theological perspective. This chapter is designed help the reader understand and articulate why evaluation in religious organizations is not an exercise in appropriating tactics from the business world but is a spiritual discipline that can stand on its own theological merits.

In chapter 3, I present four approaches to evaluation that can help a leader guide a community toward greater clarity. By presenting condition/intervention identification exercises, logic models, stakeholder maps, and evaluation rubrics, I seek to give readers a "crash course" in evaluation while also offering them an opportunity to see the connections between clarity and effective leadership.

In chapter 4, I move from evaluating or analyzing programs to planning and starting—or restarting—programs. Using some of the concepts described in chapter 3, I encourage the reader to consider how questions of clarity can be addressed before a ministry program even begins. This chapter invites the leader to consider a program from beginning to end before getting started, using evaluative practices both to avoid future pitfalls and to free up creative energy.

Chapter 5 takes us in a different direction, out of program planning and evaluation and into practical theology. It presents a faith practices approach to ministry programs in faith communities, deemphasizing programs and reintroducing holy clarity as a Christian spiritual discipline.

Finally, in the concluding chapter I consider how the work of clarification can be considered a faith practice. This chapter speaks to the question of how holy clarity can make a pastor or layperson not just a better leader but a better Christian, one more firmly grounded in God.

Each chapter includes a fictional case study related to the theory presented in that chapter. The case studies are intended to provide a jumping-off point for conversation with those who choose to read this book in small groups. Too often, evaluation is an adversarial process in which one body of individuals evaluates another with no real communication between the two. My hope for this book is that it will both celebrate and model collaborative communication. Case studies can provide grounding and entry points for group conversation. Since those presented here are fictional, group members need not worry that they will hurt someone's feelings by criticizing a character's choices. In addition to fictional cases, I use examples from my own experience and from stories I have heard. In examples, I have either changed identifiable details or amalgamated several stories together.

My motivation for writing this book came from two sources: (1) leading programs and assisting others who do so in designing evaluation strategies, and (2) teaching ministry students about the intersections between leadership in religious organizations and the practices of planning and evaluation. These two professional experiences have given me opportunities to learn about evaluation and to become familiar with some literature in the field. Teaching, leading, and consulting also put me in conversation with people who were struggling to understand what they as leaders and future leaders were expected to do by way of evaluation. Having to explain evaluation to both leaders and students, using various images and examples, helped me understand evaluation from a variety of perspectives and appreciate different learning styles.

Teaching about and consulting on evaluation have also helped me understand why evaluation can be so hard for ministerial leaders to grasp. I hope with this book to provide an accessible resource as an entry point for those who have been frustrated with either the expectations placed upon them by others or the seemingly nontheological nature of evaluative work. Although many resources are available to help leaders plan an evaluation, I believe we are just beginning to see signs that religious organizations are recognizing the unique and holy nature of evaluation in the context of a faith community.

In addition to teaching and consulting, I have served, and still serve, as a program leader myself; evaluation and all the misconceptions that come with it are familiar to me. As a doctoral student at University of Wisconsin–Milwaukee, I took my first course on program planning and evaluation during my first semester as that university's ecumenical Protestant campus minister. The ministry had fallen on hard times and was in desperate need of a strategic but radical turnaround. Planning and evaluation helped me bring about change during that first semester, but the leadership principles contained in those disciplines had a far greater impact on my work throughout my tenure in that campus ministry setting.

Written into my job description when I came to work in my current position was an explicit expectation that I would conduct a comprehensive evaluation of the field education program at Andover Newton. Having finished that assessment and having created an ongoing evaluation strategy for the field education program, I am now leading a similar process of evaluating and redesigning our school's master of divinity curriculum. Therefore, the practices I describe in this book are not merely academic to me; in many ways, I describe in this book what I do and think about every day.

Some professionals in administrative leadership refer to themselves as "evaluation experts," and many have good reason for doing so, such as technological training and experience using various research methods. I myself have some training in research methodology from my doctoral program in administrative leadership in a school of education, and I have been hired to serve as an outside evaluator for programs in religious organizations. That said, I truly believe that the best evaluations are conducted internally rather than by outside experts. But few leaders have the benefit I enjoyed of taking a course on program planning and evaluation while starting out in their jobs. Leaders within organizations need and deserve resources that help them evaluate well.

I believe that some internal evaluations conducted by untrained leaders lack neutrality and validity. In this case, an absence of validity means that the data produced do not represent reality accurately; in my experience, untrained internal evaluators do not always "hear" the truth about their organizations—either because they cannot or because participants fear repercussions if they are honest. Conversely, external evaluations conducted by consultants sometimes lack perspective. They do not always take into account institutional culture and history, since external evaluators are rarely able to invest the time and energy necessary to "get the feel" for the setting where the program takes place. Therefore, the findings of external evaluations are not "reliable"—meaning that they are not indicative or predictive of the program's impact and future success. In my own writing, teaching, and consulting, I try to correct for the weaknesses of these two extremes. I have come to believe that a leader cannot entirely outsource evaluation to consultants. My father likes to joke, "A consultant steals your watch and then tells you what time it is." Most leaders have the information before them that they need to make good decisions, but some need help in "reading their watches" so that they "know what time it is." What leaders most often need to engage in home-grown evaluation is not outside experts for every evaluative task, but rather resources and advice that help them to think in a new way.

Throughout this book I rely on training workshops, advice, and resources I received from Diane Millis, Susie Quern Pratt, and Susan Weber who have been evaluation mentors to me. I incorporate my own learning from having twice taught Ministerial Leadership in Program Planning and Evaluation at Andover Newton, experience that helped me refine my thoughts as presented here. I also make use of my experiences evaluating the ministry programs at UW–Milwaukee's University Christian Ministries and Andover Newton's field education program. Both of these have given me opportunities to learn on a deeper level how evaluation *really* works in religious organizations. I am particularly grateful to Alan McCalister, former board member and current campus minister at University Christian Ministries, and Kathryn Windsor, my colleague in field education at Andover Newton. Both helped me understand how having a conversation partner and working with teams enhances evaluative work and infuses the practice of clarification with joy.

As I said earlier, in describing my choice to include case studies in each chapter, I believe that the best reasoning takes place in community. I am fortunate to have participated in many rich communities of learning, but none has been as full of blessings as my current setting, Andover Newton Theological School. It is with gratitude for the opportunity to work with other seekers of clarity that I engage in this work of presenting my perspectives on program planning and evaluation for clarity's sake.

Chapter 1

~

Looking for Clarity in a Murky World
The Dilemma of Ministerial Leadership

THE PERSON OF FAITH WHO TRIES TO KEEP UP WITH the latest literature in ministerial leadership could not have helped noticing, over the past four or five years, an increase in the number of texts available to help a congregation with evaluation. It is hard work to evaluate pastors, ministry teams, ministry programs, and even congregations, so why might it be that so many people seem to want to read about it? Could it be that the call for accountability in education, accounting, and government has bled over into religious institutions? Or are churches beginning to see their members as "donors" rather than "tithers," contributors who want to know how their offerings are being put to work and for whose dollars the church is but one among many competitors? Or might it simply be a fad, with evaluation and appreciative inquiry and asset mapping becoming trendy tools that will soon take their place on high bookshelves, gathering dust?

What is evaluation, and what is so exciting about it that has created a market for a slew of new books on the topic? Evaluation leader Elizabeth Lynn observes that evaluation calls upon us to clarify, collect, and converse.[1] First, during an evaluation process, an organization clarifies what it seeks to accomplish. Second, the organization's leaders collect information that can help them understand the impact of their activities. Finally, leaders and constituents converse about their findings. In an evaluation I conducted at the seminary I serve, I explained our comprehensive assessment[2] process this way: "We need to start out by looking at what we say we do. Then, we need to learn what we actually do. Finally, when we find areas of discrepancy, we need to make a choice: Do we change what we say, or change what we do?"

An outside observer might look at the attention I give to assessment in my own work as a director of field education and associate dean at a seminary as a matter of "obedience." Accrediting bodies, such as the Association of Theological Schools, have made it clear that they expect assessment to get more attention than ever before at the schools for which they vouch. This expectation gives me some leverage—a good excuse—to get others on my campus to participate in assessment activities, but my motivations are more complex and personal than a desire to keep my school in good graces.

I want to promote assessment and describe it in plain language because I think that God cares whether I know what I am doing. In an institutional context, I believe God cares whether the institution's goals are noble, and God cares whether the institution's methods for reaching those goals make sense. God is pleased, I believe, when I can make connections between my activities and an outcome that makes a positive difference in the world. Therefore, I find clarification, and clarity itself, to be deeply satisfying. For me, it is a spiritual practice of purification and winnowing and discernment. It leads me to holy clarity—the theme of this book.

"Assessment for the sake of obedience" is similar to other faith practices in which a person participates in order to please but without any real conviction. Some evaluation processes take place because leaders and stakeholders seek an opportunity to grow and improve as a result of learning that takes place collaboratively. Others seek to prove something or to satisfy a requirement. Some people pray to be seen by others, and others pray to find true connection with God. As with any faith practice, an organization gets as much out of evaluation as it puts into it. Those who treat it as a fad or as "the thing to do" are unlikely to find holy clarity.

Returning to Lynn's definition of evaluation—clarify, collect, converse—we see that perhaps the simple explanation for the rising interest in the topic is the correct one: more people are reading books about evaluation because, in our world today, more of us need help in finding clarity, gathering information, and talking about what we have learned than we used to. The world in which we live is getting more and more complicated, and we need help making sense of it. There may have been a time when a person of faith could simply "eyeball" the activities of a religious institution and understand what it stood for, why it did what it did. Today we need lenses and methods and strategies for finding clarity, for on our own we cannot attain it. Like all faith practices, holy clarity is rendered elusive in a world with too much noise and too many distractions. The nature of that world, and why finding clarity in it can be difficult, is the topic for this chapter.

Kathleen Cahalan, to whose book on program planning and evaluation I give significant attention, writes, "Projects are . . . a response to a condition or set of conditions."[3] She also says that "conditions" are context-specific. When I teach students about program evaluation in ministry, I use the language of "context/intervention." If a program is an "intervention" of some kind, then we have to ask: To what condition is the intervention responding? Were we to ask what condition led to an explosion in evaluation texts for religious leaders, we would quickly discover that the world in which ministers and lay leaders now function is complicated beyond the imaginations of the founders of most religious institutions that are more than twenty years old. Evaluation, as a discipline for leadership, is emerging in response to something—a condition—and the condition continues to shape the discipline to this day.

As D. Susan Wisely, who served for more than two decades as director of program evaluation at Lilly Endowment Inc., points out, evaluation has emerged as a distinct leadership discipline over the past several decades,[4] but this evolution has not taken place in a vacuum. Over time, those who provide financial support for program initiatives have come to expect more and more information about the impact of the work they sponsor. In *Level Best: How Small and Grassroots Nonprofits Can Tackle Evaluation and Talk Results*, Marcia Festen and Marianne Philbin write, "Do not assume that because your work is urgent or even sacred, you do not need to provide evidence of competence or effectiveness. You do."[5] Of course, evaluation is healthy for leaders and the organizations they shepherd. Craig Dykstra, senior vice president for religion at Lilly Endowment Inc. writes, "Reflective practitioners of all kinds constantly build self-evaluation into the very warp and woof of their endeavors."[6] There is no separating evaluation from the work of the effective leader. For this reason, the pressure that funders place on leaders to attend to evaluation as part of their work often yields positive results. That said, when evaluation becomes a professional obligation rather than a way of thinking, leaders sometimes experience evaluation not as a reflective opportunity but rather an onerous undertaking.

The professionalization of evaluation has come as both a curse and a blessing to religious leaders. First, the curse: When an "evaluation expert" presents findings that are either not valid or not pleasing, it is easy to dismiss evaluation practices as irrelevant and damaging to institutions. Consider how much bad press evaluation is receiving in the world of education. The "No Child Left Behind" program, which increased the level of accountability for American public schools through evaluative testing, raised the hackles of educators everywhere. Colleges and universities have been threatened with the prospect of a similar quantitative evaluation method that would influence schools' abilities to gain access to federal funding. In the same academic year, two Ivy League university presidents, Drew Gilpin Faust (Harvard) and Shirley Tilghman (Princeton), spoke out against the culture of assessment in today's universities.[7] Just imagine: two university presidents speaking out against gathering information and analyzing it. Could the fear of knowing too much truly be the root of their concern? Of course not. Educators fear rather that a culture of assessment brings to America's campuses measurers of performance who know little or nothing about higher education or its mission. Leaders in liberal education, where results are notoriously hard to measure, have reason to be fearful when their institutions' supporters, including charitable foundations, seek assessment data to help them to understand the impact the institution is having on students and society.

Evaluation professionals have not always described their work in such a way that has assuaged the fears like those of presidents Faust and Tilghman. "Practitioners [of evaluation] have alternately courted and rejected the status of a science."[8] Experts in the professional practice of evaluation are given a great deal of deference and respect in today's results-oriented professional world. Some with expert-level training in evaluation might therefore find it tempting to pass themselves off as possessing an exclusive set of skills (and indeed, some have technical measurement expertise that justifies this claim), often causing those without such a background to believe that, without such special training, they are not qualified to practice evaluation.

I believe that every leader who truly wants to know what is happening in his or her institution is engaging, whether he or she realizes it, in evaluation. Leaders who wish to gather information and to make evidence-driven decisions are constantly evaluating. The problem is that, in today's world, there is simply too much information available to do this without some method or strategy at hand. I remember hearing a news story many years ago about fighter pilots and the number of instruments they needed to monitor in their cockpits. The story argued, with the help of neurological evidence, that a person can track only so many gauges at one time. Similarly, leaders can process only so much information before they start to become confused, overwhelmed, or burned out. Evaluative practices help leaders sort out all the gauges, systematizing the way they make sense of information, so that they can use the information to improve the organization.

For example, seasoned pastors know that they cannot allow one or two members of a congregation to give them "the whole story" about how a sermon was received. One or two might indicate they did not like a sermon they just heard, or that a portion of it offended them or did not strike them as true. Another one or two might say that the message was truly life-changing. But an experienced pastor knows that these comments can only hint at how the sermon was received by the congregation as a whole. A pastor would be unwise to change completely his or her preaching style and content because of a handful of comments in a receiving line. A pastor would also be mistaken if she focused all her energy on how she was received rather than on how the parishioner's faith was or was not growing with the help of faith teachings in sermons. Finding ways to sort and analyze information—both about the leader's performance and its related impact—is as important for pastors as it is for pilots.

It is quite possible, and must be pointed out, that not every leader actually wants to know what is happening in his or her institution. This thought occurred to me one day while listening to an address by long-time Boston mayor Tom Menino. I believe he was responding to some bad news, whether it was the budget or a tragedy, and he began by saying, "A leader has to face facts." I remember this snippet because it occurred to me that I have never heard a minister or a church council president define leadership in this way. Perhaps the mysterious and lofty work of ministry causes religious leaders not to use words like "facts," but I thought to myself that Menino is, whether we like it or not, correct in what he says about leadership, and church leaders must attend to this reality. The leaders of churches must face facts. But sometimes the facts are numerous, contradictory, and spin-doctored beyond what is helpful for the leader. Sometimes religious leaders pay attention to the "wrong" facts, like the board of trustees that is so obsessed with building maintenance that it forgets evangelism.

Even data that are immutably true can mislead us when not placed in the proper perspective.

Some recent literature on religious leadership has begun to point us toward the fact-facing role of the pastor. In his ground-breaking book *Making Spiritual Sense: Christian Leaders as Spiritual Interpreters,* [9] Scott Cormode argues that the primary role of the pastor is that of resident sense-maker who must bring Christian thinking to bear on the facts she or he presents. Cormode would argue that all religious leaders must face facts and help others to do so, but with a particular meaning-making system that enables them to interpret what they find. He would say that the leader uses spiritual paradigms for analyzing facts, sorting them according to faith principles. Robert Dale, in his book *Leadership for a Changing Church: Charting the Shape of the River,* [10] written ten years earlier, makes the claim that, whereas industrial-age (twentieth-century) leaders made products or things, information-age (twenty-first-century) leaders make sense or meaning. These two authors both point to the sense-making, meaning-making responsibilities of a leader, and Menino points to the fact-facing duties related to leadership. All three help us understand why evaluation is important: evaluation as a leadership practice seeks to expose the inner workings and inconsistencies of programs and institutions. If we use evaluation as Lynn argues—to clarify our missions, collect information about our impact, and talk within our organization about how we can be more effective—we can see that evaluation is a sense-making, fact-facing tool integral to the work of the leader.

When I was in seminary, a guest preacher in chapel[11] who was approximately five years into ministry offered a sermon on the model of ministry that was helping her to lead. She described the mental framework that defined her ministry in its first three years as that of "historian-lover." As she took leadership in a struggling urban congregation, she took it upon herself to learn everything she could about where the church had been and to love it and every member with all her heart. I found her sermon helpful and memorable on three levels. First, she described having a mental model for who she was as the leader of a faith community at a particular time. In a complicated world, religious leaders need to define their roles carefully to themselves and to others. Second, her model was open to change. The historian-lover model was helpful when the church was struggling, but as the church began to thrive, she chose a model that captured some of the same sentiment as Cormode's model of the leader as spiritual sense-maker. Third, I found the sermon helpful because it argued in favor of the leader's knowing the context well. Evaluative practices help us do this, and having that knowledge is the beginning of clarity.

The world does not make as much sense as it used to, and leaders today need more sense-making help than ever before. As we explore the nature of postmodern society, we will see how the murky world in which we live requires special strategies and practices for making clarity a reality.

The Postmodern World

Before we can explore clarification as a leadership practice, even as a spiritual practice, we must first consider why clarity is in such short supply in religious organizations today. Even the smallest congregations can feel chaotic, undisciplined, and confused about where to turn their attention. This confusion has something to do with postmodernism, its effects on religious organizations, and the challenges—such as "*de facto* congregationalism"[12] and resistance to administrative leadership—that postmodernism poses for today's religious leaders.

When I talk with seminary students about postmodernism, I usually begin by noting how complicated our culture has become, and by suggesting that understanding postmodernism can show us why. Without fail, a student interrupts me mid-thought and asks me to define postmodernism. Of course, that was what I was just about to do, but perhaps because the term is used so freely without definition, students are desperate for a working definition. My reaction to these interruptions is twofold: first, I promise students that they will get their definition, but that they probably will not be satisfied, as postmodernism is a term and a societal condition that resists definition. Second, I observe that both the question the student poses and the pace at which the class hopes the question will be answered say a great deal about postmodernism. The student's question thus becomes a metaphor for postmodernism itself. The cultural era of postmodernism resists definition; it is one in which reality is defined by individuals rather than by one monolithic societal voice, and in which truth is negotiable. It is also a time when there is "no speed limit,"[13] when information flies at us faster than we can process it, and when we become accustomed to rapid responses and quick (if unsatisfactory) solutions. The cultural age in which ministerial leaders function is both rich with opportunity and hard to understand. By the very definition of the term "postmodernism," I cannot define it, but I can describe some of its contours as they relate to the work of leading a faith community.

The postmodern era began in about the 1960s with the collapse of the industrial age. The term *postmodern* refers to an antecedent modern age, which arguably started with the Enlightenment, or the philosophical movement in the nineteenth century that lifted up human potential and accomplishment as all-powerful and limitless. So when we talk about postmodernism, we are contrasting our era with the age that emerged out of the Enlightenment and ended sometime after the 1950s, when a worldview that believed human potential was limitless began to break down.

Many authors who have written about postmodernism and religious organizations (in this chapter, I rely most heavily on Robert Dale and Jill Hudson) remember and experienced the 1960s. Not having lived through that period myself, I realize that my perspective on postmodernism is shaped by my having spent my entire conscious life in the era and not having personally had to adjust to its challenges. The social conditions I describe have always been with me. Yet I realize that postmodernism, a liminal or in-between time, is best described using contrasts. Most scholars and social commentators who describe postmodernism chart out a cultural path from certainty to uncertainty, from clarity to unclarity.

In the modern era, certain truths were taken for granted. The most obvious ones were that knowledge is always good, and that human beings can achieve anything. Truth was understood to be singular, nonnegotiable, and attainable. Religion as a resource for meaning-making gave way to science as a more powerful tool for such investigation; religious institutions ceded the discovery of truth to the scientific community. In the postmodern era, beginning most noticeably in the resistance movements of the 1960s, such as the civil rights movement and women's liberation, the limits of human knowledge were becoming apparent. These movements taught us that cultural definitions of reality were shaped in large part by power: "truth" defined by women or people of color was different from "truth" as defined by white men in positions of authority. As these versions of truth came in contact with one another, and as all these perspectives on the nature of reality began to find their places in civic discourse, monolithic presentations of truth began to fall apart. Furthermore, wars, technological advances that brought more harm than good, and the limitations of science all caused the modern era's self-assured humanism to blur at the edges, and then to begin to disintegrate at the center.

The postmodern era is characterized by the following:

1. New populations seek a public voice and positions of power.
2. Computers and other technologies lead to a manifold increase in the rate of societal change.
3. Human knowledge is found to be inadequate to address ethical issues, such as ecological crises and human reproduction.

Related to these characteristics of the postmodern era are three new ways in which human beings engage the institutions of which they are part. In our postmodern era:

1. What is "true" is now a matter of discussion and debate. Conflicting understandings of reality coexist within single communities, and truth is defined by individuals rather than by communities or society.
2. There are no agreed-upon rules for how people are to interact with each other or the society, no "speed limit"[14] for their engagement.
3. Knowledge and progress are not always viewed as "good."[15]

There is much good news to be found for religious institutions in the postmodern era. First, whereas the modern era gave central authority to science, the postmodern era has made room for many simultaneous perspectives on meaning. This shift gives more space for faith-oriented thinking. When one need not choose between science and religion to think about the meaning of life, religious leaders find that there is again a space at the table for them in ethical discussion and public conversations. In the modern era, religion was relegated to the world of superstition; institutions of higher education founded by the church were, slowly and methodically, taken over by humanistic scholars who sidelined religious leaders. Today, in an effort to find ways to bring religious ways of meaning back into the academy, those same institutions are revisiting the structures they broke apart.

When there is good news, however, there is almost always related bad news. Even though multiple ways of seeking truth are now welcome at the highest levels of societal meaning-making, religious institutions still have an adjustment on their hands. For even though there is more room in the postmodern era for religious thinking, most religious institutions were built on modern principles. That many churches have not meaningfully revisited their assumptions, infrastructures, governance styles, and leadership practices since before the end of the modern era leaves these institutions unable to address the realities of a postmodern age. Consider these two defeated assumptions:

"Normal, decent people go to church." This statement might have been true in the early part of the twentieth century, but one characteristic of the postmodern era is that "rules" are not agreed upon universally. Individuals are given more freedom to define their realities and to decide what rules make sense for them and their families. For the church, this shift is not necessarily good news. American culture has moved away from a time when it was assumed that all went to church, when it was just a matter of where and not whether the family was part of a church, to a time when churches have had to learn to attract people. Ministers whose seminaries trained them to receive people now must learn to recruit congregants, and to help leaders in the congregation evangelize when evangelism might not have been part of the community's self-understanding.

Having been born after the end of the modern era, I do not remember a time when the reality I have just described did not exist. But I work regularly with pastors for whom this change has been an adjustment. At a clergy gathering I attended several years ago, one of my older colleagues stated that he could not imagine encouraging a gifted young person to enter the ordained ministry today, because the work of having to get people to think about going to church *at all* was not something he had signed up for. It occurred to me, and to some other slightly younger members of the clergy at this gathering, that we had an advantage in that the "rules" had not been changed on us. We entered seminary realizing that religious participation had become optional for even the finest and most upstanding citizens in our communities. Because we did not have to adjust to this change, we were perhaps not as disillusioned as some of our more experienced colleagues, and in fact we found some freedom in knowing that members of our congregations would not be there if they did not want to be.

A second debunked assumption: "My faith community is located in a large building at the center of town." In New England, where I live and serve, this assumption is dying hard. Many New England towns have huge church edifices that are centrally located and that hold four hundred people when filled to capacity but where fewer than forty worship on most Sundays. And yet recent studies indicate that the United States is still a strikingly religious country. How can that be? Megachurches cannot account for the statistics. Rather, religious participation has taken on new meanings and patterns. Faith communities meet online and in storefronts and in homes. Some people of faith have no discernible hunger for a faith community; rather they read spiritual books and watch worship services on television. Postmodern faith is more individualistic than its modern predecessor, and it is less predictable. Pastors often find themselves in conversations with members of their wider communities who say that they are deeply spiritual but not religious; pastors find it difficult to respond to those statements, because their leadership depends upon affiliation with just such a community that the spiritual-but-not-religious seem to find unnecessary.

The institutions where the minister's leadership is rooted often took shape during the modern era and have not experienced meaningful change since then. They are governed by standing committees that move methodically and slowly, even when significant issues (such as rapid membership decline) arise. Their budgets are based on what the church has done in the past, not on what it might do in the future. Their leadership structures are hierarchical, often with the pastor at the head, even in congregational polities. They interpret conflict as a problem to be fixed; they interpret popular culture as an enemy to their cause. Few leaders in religious institutions feel prepared to engage in conversation with someone who thinks that the institutional church is simply unnecessary, but such conversations are the wave of the future in a postmodern church world.

This might seem rather a bleak picture, but it is giving way, just as the modern era gave way. The postmodern era is no longer a "new age," as is evidenced by the number of pastors now serving who are too young to remember the modern era. Churches are finding ways to adapt to the postmodern era, sometimes by adopting a whole new way of being church, and sometimes by adapting their structures to a fast-changing, less rule-bound, more interconnected society. Here are some markers of churches that have begun to adapt to the postmodern context:

1. Their committee structures are more nimble. For example, teams of leaders with particular gifts are assembled to address specific issues.

2. Their budgets are based, at least primarily, upon the churches' understanding of their future mission and their calling.

3. Their leadership structure is a flat hierarchy, in which different leaders have the last word depending upon the issue at hand, and the pastor plays a coordinating and collaborating role with those leaders, bringing a spiritual perspective on the work of the church. Thus, the last word comes not from a committee or a leader, but from God as interpreted by the community under the leadership of the pastor.

4. They understand conflict to be a teacher and an illuminator of the path God has laid before them, and they have decision-making structures that help the church move forward—rather than freezing—when conflict arises.

5. They understand themselves to be a part of the culture, providing an alternative worldview (a faith perspective) that both participates in and critiques the wider society. They understand the church to have a crucial role in society, providing a Christian framework for making sense of the world, and they interact with culture meaningfully, critically, and with an openness to changing themselves as church just as they seek to change culture through the church.

Just as we can see contrasts between modern-era churches and churches that are adapting to postmodern realities, we can see differences between modern and postmodern ministerial leadership styles. As a teacher of ministerial leadership in a seminary, I am keenly aware of how different the skills and cognitive abilities of ministers in a postmodern era need to be from those of their predecessors. But I also recognize that modern expectations of ministerial leaders still abound. Modern-era leaders knew the "product" they were expected to generate and developed skills around these products. They needed to know their Bibles, understand theology, and be able to perform functions, such as conducting various forms of worship services. In their leadership they were able to rely on linear progression between planning and implementation of programs. Stewardship drives, membership drives, and special events went like "clockwork," in that they happened on the same schedule from year to year. In some settings, these patterns are still in place, and ministers need to be ready for them. But they also have to be ready for much more.

Even in settings where the work of the ministerial leader appears simple and structured, much has changed under the surface. Ministers need to know and accept that multiple expectations of the role of the leader exist at all times. The very definition of the role of a pastor, a church council chair, or a deacon will vary enormously within one faith community. Leaders must therefore be more relational, emotionally intelligent, and inclusive than ever before. "Answers" like "We do this because we have always done this" will drive away postmodern thinkers seeking a faith community.

The pastor in a faith community adapting to postmodernism must behave more like a sheepdog than a shepherd.[16] The sheepdog keeps the flock together, as both the sheepdog and the sheep seek to follow where the shepherd is leading them. The sheepdog has to consider the various directions in which the sheep tend to wander, anticipate their meanderings, and motivate them to move toward the shepherd's destination. Like the sheep, however, the sheepdog does not speak the shepherd's language, nor does the sheepdog have insight into where the shepherd might want to go. Therefore, sheep and sheepdog alike must remain open.

Effective postmodern leaders function more like sheepdogs than shepherds. They also must be visionary, looking more toward their future calling than to the past. They must be selective as they develop their mental models for ministry (like the "historian-lover" I mentioned previously), in that they will likely be bombarded constantly with expectations and new ideas for the faith community. They must be skilled interpersonally, building relationships, fostering consensus, and encouraging buy-in to the vision they and their communities have shaped together. One might ask, "Can any of these skills be taught?" The answer is yes, but seminary educators must be as nimble as their pastoral counterparts in determining the right ways to teach such elusive skills, which are more "arts" than "crafts."

Postmodern religious leaders must be rooted and grounded spiritually, in that the constant change in postmodern America will overwhelm them if they do not have a strong faith life and a God-centered vision that transcends the many voices they hear. They must be humble enough to learn from their mistakes, for so much of their sailing takes place in uncharted waters that they must not be hard on themselves when their best-laid plans do not lead to the hoped-for outcomes. They must see themselves as servants of the community more than as commanders-in-chief, while also retaining respect and authority so that they can motivate the community toward its vision when a few voices of dissent seek to take it off course. Just the ability to distinguish between those few distracting voices of dissent and those that provide useful differing perspectives requires a high level of interpersonal acuity and relational talent.

In her book *When Better Isn't Enough: Evaluation Tools for the 21st-Century Church*,[17] Jill Hudson offers twelve characteristics of ministerial leaders who can thrive in the postmodern church. Two that come as a surprise to some readers are, first, that the postmodern leader must be comfortable with technology, and second, that she or he must be familiar with change theory. Many pastors do not know how to make use of technology in their ministries, and somehow this shortcoming is regarded in some settings as normal and acceptable. Hudson believes that a minister cannot serve a church in today's world without using technology. I agree. It would be unheard of for a pastor to say that she chooses not to use a telephone and therefore will not return any phone calls. Yet pastors often reject e-mail and the Web and achieve the same results as if they did not return phone calls: losing touch with the community they are supposed to be serving.

Hudson writes, and Dale concurs, that the ability to lead in the midst of change is essential for the postmodern leader. Hudson argues that leaders must know something about change theory, because change is hard on both people and institutions, and leaders must understand something about why this is so in order to help both people and churches through such difficulties. Dale writes that leaders must be able to charge ahead into uncertain territory while also loving the people, rather than becoming angry with them when their anxiety gets the better of them.[18]

The religious leader in a postmodern world must engage in the following practices, to name a few:

1. Make decisions inclusively and transparently.
2. Minimize anxiety about change while also maintaining an appropriate level of urgency.[19]
3. Listen to dissent but keep the vision at the forefront.
4. Articulate the community's vision clearly and often.[20]
5. Use spiritual language and images in doing so, to help make sense[21] of the complex world in which we live.

All of these practices require effort, training, and experience. They also require a model for ministry that includes an understanding that part of ministry is leadership. Often people of faith misunderstand the difference between chaplaincy and leadership:

A chaplain provides spiritual care, whereas a ministerial leader works with a community to help it shape a vision for its calling, and then the leader helps the community work toward that vision. Although some institutional chaplains play a leadership role, they are not "in charge" of the institution, but rather provide care within it. A chaplaincy approach alone will not be sufficient for leading a faith community.

In my experience, many laypeople assume that pastors both understand themselves to be community leaders and have training to help them to live into this role. In reality, questions abound regarding the appropriate leadership role of the pastor in a congregation. This confusion can frustrate pastors who believe they are expected both to act as confident decision makers and to ask permission before doing virtually anything new. But the ambiguity has the hidden benefit of making space for innumerable models of leadership in ministry: many leadership styles can find success in ministry today. Just as the stereotype that pastors must all be male, straight, and married with children is breaking down, the assumption that ministerial leaders are all charismatic and extroverted no longer holds either. Some pastors are more collaborative, and some are more authoritative, but many models can work.

It seems that, style aside, confusion about the role of the ministerial leader as an administrator remains problematic. Left over from the modern era are certain assumptions about the pastor's role in leading worship and caring for the congregation pastorally. What seems to be truly "up for grabs" is a common understanding of the ordained minister's leadership role in governance and administration; those expectations vary widely and leave both lay and ordained leaders confused about where authority is located. If we understand the ministerial leader to have an important role in helping an organization find holy clarity, we can see how ambiguity about the administrative leadership role of the pastor might influence evaluation. If the pastor is charged with a leadership role, sense-making becomes part of his or her expected functioning. If there is a lack of clarity about what the pastor is meant to be doing, how can that pastor then bring clarity to a community?

Obstacles to Sense-Making in Today's Churches

I have an astigmatism, so I wear glasses at all times. When I have to take them off, even for a short time—say, when I take my daughter swimming—I feel disoriented and disconnected. It is fair to say that most people feel most at ease and grounded when they can see clearly what is taking place around them. Holy clarity in ✗ religious organizations is like clear vision: When it is attained, the community feels the peace and security that come with seeing what is happening, even if what it sees is imperfect and in need of improvement. Evaluation practices can help a leader establish that clarity. Considering that human beings by nature want to see clearly, we could reasonably ask why not all religious organizations dig with gusto into evaluative practices that could help them achieve clarity. Yet it is common for leaders in all institutions to resist evaluation, and here are some reasons why:

1. They do not truly want to know what is happening, for they fear what they might discover.
2. They think that they already know all there is to know about their organizations, and that they will not find any new information.
3. They have participated in formal evaluative processes in the past and found them unhelpful.
4. They think of evaluation as a wedge for making unpopular decisions, and they do not wish to engage in the evaluation or the decisions for fear of conflict.
5. They find evaluation to be corporate-minded, not intended for the church, and not appropriate in a sacred community.
6. They believe that any effort the faith community makes

should be celebrated for the mere fact that it is happening;
whether the effort is leading the community toward a vision is not as important as the effort invested.

7. Because of uncertainty about the appropriate leadership
   role of lay and ordained ministers, no one is certain who
   should be evaluating whom.

8. As mentioned previously, those without formal training in
   evaluation believe they are not qualified to carry out evaluation processes, so they place their attention elsewhere.

As both a colleague and a consultant, I have worked with some
leaders who have come to resist evaluation for good reasons. They
have participated in, and have been subjected to, evaluations that
were conducted poorly and for all the wrong reasons. But I have
also seen potential for opening minds that have been closed to
evaluation when leaders start to take advantage of the tools that
evaluators have developed to find true clarity. I have also seen
leaders who have embraced evaluation practices become not just
better evaluators, but better leaders overall, and particularly better
administrative leaders.

The work of pastoral ministry is rich and complex. It calls upon
us to interpret, communicate, lead, cross barriers, counsel, speak
truth to power, and educate. One of the most exciting aspects of
ministry for me is the diversity of the work and the fact that no
two days in ordained ministry are ever exactly the same. The practice of evaluation, if one were to categorize it among the varied
arts of ministry, falls into the realm of "administrative leadership."
Although I argue throughout this book that evaluation embodies
a sacred practice of holy clarification, evaluation takes place both
formally and informally through systems, structures, and activities
that must be planned and implemented. One overarching obstacle
to evaluation, and therefore to holy clarity, is this: administrative
leadership in ministry is among the least developed, appreciated,
understood, and agreed-upon ministerial art forms.

This view is held particularly by ordained ministers, but it is not limited to them. Two books that interpret findings from the comprehensive Pulpit & Pew[22] study point to administrative leadership as a crucial and contended area of practice for ministers today. Gregory Jones and Kevin Armstrong write that many ministerial leaders encounter tension, both their own and their communities',

> *because of our ambivalence about power and authority, or perhaps to rebel against them because of the way in which management theories and bureaucratic expectations have afflicted the contemporary church's self-understanding. However, the root for the term "administration" is the same as for "ministry," and the question is not whether pastors will provide administrative leadership—it is whether it will be done well or poorly.* [23]

In *God's Potters: Pastoral Leadership and Shaping Congregations*, Jackson Carroll writes about some of the cultural realities ministerial leaders face.[24] Although he does not explore postmodernism at great length, his arguments help us understand some of postmodernism's implications for ministerial leaders. He states that today's world is not necessarily a more difficult ministry setting in which to serve as a pastor, but that it is different from what many are used to, from what many were trained to function in. Among the many areas he explores, relying on data from Pulpit & Pew research, two stand out when one considers administrative leadership and ministry:

1. What some have called "*de facto* congregationalism,"[25] in which the laity want and expect a high level of input in the institutions of which they are a part, and
2. A culture of consumerism, in which church participants tend to view religion as a commodity like any other.

In a church climate where all participants want and expect to have a say, ministerial leaders need to gather input in ways that are transparent, healthy, fair to all, and accurate. At the same time, members of religious organizations often see themselves not as co-leaders or participants but as consumers. They wish to engage their leaders in a transactional manner, contributing resources in exchange for services. Religious leaders can find these two competing claims—a desire for full participation coupled with an expectation of fee-for-service responsiveness—to be confusing to the point that they wish to withdraw from activities where expectations like these might be placed upon them.

Clergy in particular rarely make administration their top priority for three reasons:

1. A phenomenon I call "the pietistic fantasy," which romanticizes notions that ministry is qualitatively different from other kinds of jobs and relegates administrative leadership to the category of "unworthy."

2. An intellectual and religious heritage in Western civilization privileges the life of the mind over the life of action. Parker Palmer, in his book *The Active Life*, [26] writes of classical Greek distinctions between the life of the mind and the life of activity: the life of the mind was regarded as more lofty and worthy. Since Greek influences pervade religious traditions and Western civilization as a whole, it is to be expected that such hierarchies persist.

3. A culture within ministry that permits, even encourages, disdain for administrative tasks, even the ones essential to the functioning of a community, such as returning calls and maintaining an accurate calendar.

As I mentioned earlier, it often surprises me that pastors admit that they do not enjoy administrative tasks. One rarely hears an ordained minister say she or he does not like to preach, visit sick people, or lead Bible studies, although surely there are clergy who like and dislike those tasks to varying degrees. A student told me recently about an event where a minister said of administrative tasks and money in her church, "If it's not in my ordination vows, I refuse to do it, and I don't see anything in those vows about the stewardship campaign." This was a pastor whose work was considered so exemplary that she was invited to speak to a seminary class. This mentality presents an obstacle to even talking about clergy's administrative leadership in churches.

As I said earlier, these confounding realities related to administrative leadership in ministry are not limited to clergy. Lay leaders in congregations both compound the confusion pastors feel about the role of administrative leadership and experience their own ambivalence, making evaluation as an administrative function a hard sell among numerous hard sells.

One way that lay leaders reinforce the stereotype is by accepting it as par for the course that a pastor's administrative skills are poor. One need only think back to beloved Father Mulcahy of the television show *M*A*S*H* to know that clergy are not always expected to possess practical abilities, and some ministers play into this stereotype, choosing not to learn to use the copy machine, so no one minds when they delegate such tasks to others. Bungling ministers are culturally accepted, whereas a bungling accountant is an accountant no one would hire. This acceptance of administrative ineptitude carries hidden dangers, however, as it sets up the notion that ministers do only lofty work, which can have the further negative side effect of telling other leaders in the church that they cannot participate in the work of ministry.

Ordained ministers who abdicate their administrative leadership role to the lowest possible rung on the ladder of priorities can create confusion for other leaders. For example, lay ministers who, although not ordained, serve full-time in ministry are left unsure as to whether they have the authority to provide administrative leadership. They may think that, without the imprimatur of ordination, it would be inappropriate for them to take a leadership role in evaluation, but since the pastor does not prioritize the work, it ultimately does not take place. Similarly, laypeople who volunteer in ministry through volunteer boards look to the pastor to define how much attention ought to be devoted to administrative tasks. Although the best ministries are structured in such a way that administration is part of, but does not overshadow, ministry,[27] laypeople often feel that they do not have sufficient authority to take the lead in evaluation. Like pastors, they would rather participate in ministry than in administration,[28] but at the same time their ministries cannot function without planning and evaluation. They look to the pastor to set the tone, and the tone the pastor sets often indicates that evaluation is not central to the effectiveness of the religious organization.

Therefore, numerous forces prevent religious organizations from seeking clarity. Conspiring with predispositions to avoid administrative tasks in general and potentially controversial tasks in particular reflects misguided assumptions about what evaluation is and what it is meant to accomplish. Cahalan[29] offers several faulty assumptions about evaluation for religious organizations:

1. It consists of gathering feedback immediately after an event.
2. It adds work onto an already full portfolio of responsibilities for the leader.
3. It requires experts.
4. It is challenging, even dangerous, in that it might expose realities that lead to change, or at least to hard questions.

In their book *Level Best: How Small and Grassroots Nonprofits Can Tackle Evaluation and Talk Results*,[30] Festen and Philbin provide a countervailing rationale for evaluation whose strength outweighs the worries to which Cahalan points. Although they agree that leaders' misunderstanding about what evaluation is and can be certainly provides disincentive for investing time and resources in evaluation, they make a compelling case that today's leader does not have the luxury of saying that evaluation takes too much time away from other activities or will not be a leadership priority. They argue that instinct is not enough; donors want to protect their investments and reputations. Constituents want clear information about how an organization of which they are a part is making a difference. Legislators—or in the church's case, denominational bodies—want oversight. The media want facts. Leaders who cannot provide this clarity cannot thrive in today's complicated world. Leaders who rely on just one set of "instruments," their two eyes and their two ears, will not have sufficient information to satisfy these crucial stakeholders in the life of a religious institution.

In the Nick Hornby novel *High Fidelity*,[31] the main character, Rob, is a man nearing middle age who is always in and out of love. He sabotages good relationships, saying he relies on his instincts in matters of romance. When he starts to realize how lonely and isolated his so-called instincts are causing him to be, he offers a soliloquy, saying he is ready to make a change: "I've been thinking with my guts... and frankly speaking... I have come to the conclusion that my guts have s--- for brains." Many ministerial leaders think from their guts—or even better, from their hearts. This tendency is both necessary and appropriate for one living into a sacred calling. But, much like Rob, ministers often suffer for relying only on their guts and trusting their instincts too much in a complicated world. Evaluative practices are not intended to strip ministry of that gut-feeling, heart-following style of leadership. Rather, they give us tools that enhance our instincts, helping us use more than our guts and hearts to learn about our ministry settings. Evaluative practices keep us humble, for they constantly remind us that we do not know everything, even about ministries we serve day in and day out. These practices are built upon the notion that our perspective is just that, *our* perspective—not the only one, and not the perfect one.

One of the most important characteristics a leader can possess is humility. When leaders understand themselves to be imperfect and broken like all other human beings, they are better able to connect with other people and to place their trust in God. As I said earlier, leaders in religious organizations make the mistake of thinking that they know all there is to know about the quality and the impact of their work. This assumption lacks humility and overrelies on human strength. Good leaders and good evaluators know better than to think that there are no surprises or mysteries hidden within their ministries. To accept this reality with humility is a first step toward finding holy clarity. The next step is to create good strategies for exploring and discovering those mysteries, and evaluative practices can help in those efforts.

Case Study: The Church Fair

Overton Park Church loves its late-November fair. Since the early 1950s, the Women's Guild of the church has worked for six months each year planning fair activities, gathering donations for the rummage sale, coordinating volunteers to cook, and inviting local craftspeople to sell their wares at the fair. Between food, the rummage sale, and table rentals, the church has raised at least ten thousand dollars and sometimes, when the weather has been good, up to thirteen thousand.

Pastor Karen Fuller and her co-pastor and husband, Mike Fuller, came to serve Overton Park three years ago. Mike works part-time in the church and part-time as a staff writer for a Christian magazine. The couple live in the parsonage, and Mike writes from home. Karen and Mike were invited to attend the fair the first year, and to the delight of guild members they did so. In the second year, they volunteered to help with food. It was after that fair that Karen and Mike began, privately, to share concerns about the fair and its role in the life of the church.

On the surface, the fair had never been better. It always drew a large attendance and served as a kickoff event for Overton Park's festive Advent season. The crafter who sold Christmas wreaths at the fair was allowed to use his table for free in exchange for providing wreaths to decorate the church. Church members hung them during worship in a special and cherished ritual on the first Sunday of Advent. Best of all, the fair was the one community-wide event that the church hosted each year. At first, Karen and Mike viewed it as an opportunity for evangelism.

Their concerns might have seemed trivial to some, but Karen and Mike feared that the issues they saw might lead to trouble in the future. First, they learned that the fair proceeds were used to make up for budget shortfalls in the church and had been used this way for many years. In the fair's early years, up until the 1970s or so, the Women's Guild had used the proceeds to support local charities. Many in the church still believed that this was the practice and did not realize that proceeds were now used only within the church. Karen in particular believed that if some church members and townspeople realized that the fair funds were used to cover general operating expenses, they would be upset. When Karen broached the subject with a guild member, suggesting that some clarification might be appropriate, she received a chilly, defensive response.

Second, it was clear that the guild had control over the fair planning and that newcomers (including the two new pastors) were not invited to have input. At one point in the life of the church, this arrangement was positive; the church board members were all men, and the guild and its fair were the area of the church where women had control. But the generation gap in the guild was noticeable; no younger women, except for daughters of guild members, were invited to participate in the planning or carrying out of the fair. Younger women in the church tended to gravitate toward the book group or the Sunday school. Any new member who had an interest in helping with the fair was given an opportunity to volunteer but only under the leadership of one of the guild members. Some found it quaint to take (often stern) orders from octogenarians, but most of the younger women were not interested in giving time to this kind of activity. In turn, those same octogenarians were disappointed that few younger women pitched in, blaming their absence on the fact that many women in the church were working outside the home.

Karen and Mike were working with church leaders on a "visioning process" for the congregation. In the early conversations they had had with deacons, religious educators, and music leaders, the fair had not come up in conversation. Mike suggested that he and Karen sit down and talk with the Women's Guild members about the guild, the fair, and that group's vision for the future of the church. It seemed a good idea at the time, but when Karen phoned a guild member (not the person with whom she had raised the question of transparency in fund usage) to explore whether she and Mike might come to a portion of the guild's next meeting, an awkward silence ensued. The woman, who had always been friendly toward Karen in the past, said that she would need to talk with other guild members before extending such an invitation, as pastors who had served the church in the past had never before wanted to "interfere" in the fall fair.

Discussion Questions

- Do you think Karen and Mike's concerns about the fair are valid? Why or why not?
- What cultural changes do you believe underlie this turn of events in Overton Park Church?
- What do you make of Karen's approach when she asked about the use of fair funds? Would you have approached the question in the same way or differently? Why?
- What might have been your next move if you had had a phone conversation like the one that ended this case?

Chapter 2

~

The Holiness of Clarity
Why Does Clarity Matter to God?

AT ANDOVER NEWTON I TEACH A COURSE TITLED
"Ministerial Leadership in Program Planning and Evaluation."
Last year, a lay auditor—I will call her "Beth"—who works for a
denomination's regional office took the course and participated
mostly as an observer. After about the fourth week, I gave a lecture
titled "Theology and Program Planning and Evaluation," in which
I shared with students my thoughts on the holy nature of clarity
and how evaluative practices can help leaders find it. Beth raised
her hand during the question-and-answer session and offered the
other students some thoughts on why this topic is so important to
ministerial leaders today.

Part of Beth's role in her office includes administering emergency grants to churches in crisis. She is responsible for determining whether a church's situation meets the standards for the grants
and then making sure that the church completes necessary reports
after it receives funding. Beth described the frustration she experiences with many of these dealings. Often the leaders who call her
do not read the standards for grants before getting in touch, and
when asked to articulate their church's specific needs, they speak
in vague terms. Beth said that church leaders were seldom able
to articulate compellingly why they needed assistance, what they
would do with funds if they had them, and how they would know

and demonstrate that the emergency assistance was successful in getting the congregation through a tough situation.

When Beth would ask them to clarify their proposals and present resources such as logic models (which I will describe in the next chapter), the church leaders with whom she spoke often threw up their hands in frustration. They accused Beth of behaving too much like a businesswoman in the face of a true crisis. "Why don't you have faith in us and in God?" they would ask. Beth told the students that they, as future ministers, needed to understand that they would have to be able to articulate clearly the purpose and goals of the institutions they would serve. They also, she said, would need to demonstrate the Christian significance of the ability to describe a clear vision. Beth laid out a twofold challenge that ministerial leaders face in an increasingly complex world: First, they need to be able to describe clearly the work and purpose of religious organizations. Second, they must show communities—both internal and external—that this purpose and the clarity with which it is described have deep theological roots.

When people of faith dismiss leadership practices from the secular world as "too businesslike," they often do so out of a need for a break from the materialistic, consumption-obsessed culture in which they live. They seek an alternative form of community in their churches, a form governed not by transactions but by unconditional love. When participants—and sometimes leaders—in religious organizations hear the word "evaluation," they assume that the practice must (1) be on loan from the business world, and (2) have a "bottom line" that is, at some level, materialistic. "For how can human redemption and transformation be evaluated or measured?" they might ask. In this chapter I address the first of those misconceptions: that evaluation is, at its root, borrowed from the business world. Evaluators in religious organizations need only look to sacred Scripture and basic theological principles to see that the Christian faith tradition provides ample justification for evaluative practices in religious organizations. In chapter 3, I move on to describe ways in which organizations can define success in spiritual terms.

Cross-pollination between the secular business world and religious organizations can be beneficial to both realms. Susan Weber, of the Indianapolis Center for Congregations, is a certified trainer in the discipline of Appreciative Inquiry, and when she went to Case Western Reserve University for her coursework, she was surprised to see the overlap between that discipline and the work of ministry. At this business school, Weber learned to ask engaging questions while listening with compassion. She came away convinced that Appreciative Inquiry has, perhaps without direct knowledge, borrowed heavily from spiritual direction and other faith-oriented ways of knowing and learning. Now, through leaders like Weber, the church is "borrowing back" methods like Appreciative Inquiry.

We can find biblical and theological appreciation for clarity, truth-seeking, and sharp insight in both sacred texts and the teachings of the early church. In significant ways, the secular world borrowed this appreciation and used it to create stronger companies with robust bottom lines. John Calvin was perhaps the first to connect Christian faith overtly with secular striving, and since the spread of his writings about what we now call the "Protestant work ethic," business and religious organizations have shared a history in their conduct. Now, in our complex age, religious leaders have an opportunity to revisit ancient and sacred stories to motivate themselves and their communities to find greater clarity for their missions and activities.

Holy Clarity: We Know It When We See It

Much like "postmodernism," the term "holy clarity" is difficult to define without the benefit of juxtaposition. Imagine that you, at the invitation of a colleague from work, are attending a fundraising event for a charitable organization about which you know little. During dessert, the executive director gives a fifteen-minute speech that includes a pitch, asking attendees to become more involved and to give generously. If he clearly states (1) the change the organization seeks to promote in society, (2) the activities that will lead to the change, and (3) the resources that will make the change possible, you come away from the evening feeling, if not convicted to become more invested, at least satisfied that you have contributed to a good cause through attending the event. If he offers only a few examples of what the organization does, speaks in vague terms about needing to change the world, and gives no insight into what someone like you could do to get involved, you leave the event feeling confused and empty. Even if you do not drive home thinking, "I wish he had been clearer," you are not likely to seek avenues to provide greater support, because that lack of clarity quietly repels you.

Why might this be? Why might a potential advocate for an organization be driven away from participation simply because the leader of the organization was insufficiently clear? Perhaps the answer is simple: you do not get more involved because you do not know how. And surely there is merit to that hypothesis. On a deeper level, however, I believe that human beings crave clarity. They need it, they find it beautiful, and they are attracted to it. Leaders who can help others to see clearly have tremendous power to motivate others. As I write this chapter, Barack Obama is on the cusp of securing the Democratic presidential nomination. One of the critiques Hillary Clinton's campaign leveled against Obama was that he had done little more than give a handful of good speeches so far in his career. I argue that Americans have at times responded passionately to Obama because he speaks clearly. His words make sense to them, and this clear communication captivates them. Although clarification is not always holy—for some leaders manipulate information to suit their interests and call their work clarification—clarity is important to people now and is becoming more so as the world changes. In this complicated postmodern era, the leader who can work with people to make sense of what is happening around them will wield tremendous power. The leader need not be a great performer, a confident speechmaker, or even a highly intelligent thinker. She need only be able to imagine what might be confusing to people, help them recognize the unclarity around them, and give them a vision of the possible.

There are four theological themes upon which a leader in a religious organization can build a community-wide appreciation for clarity as a sacred state of being:

1. The inherent value of truth telling.
2. The intrinsic beauty of clarity.
3. The juxtaposition of blindness versus sight, both spiritual and physical.
4. The perfect clarity in the kingdom of God.

I present these theological perspectives to provide the religious leader with a repertoire from which to draw when she or he seeks to motivate a faith community toward finding greater clarity, using, where appropriate, methods—whether developed in the secular world or not—associated with program planning and evaluation.

The Value of Truth Telling[1]

One of the central purposes of evaluation is to uncover the truth about an organization's activities and impact. Are the activities running smoothly? Is the infrastructure supporting those activities sufficient to the organization's tasks? Are the programs having the intended effect on participants or the community? Evaluative practices are important because sometimes the truth is hard to find without disciplined exploration. At other times, leaders need to rely on evaluative practices to overcome not just their blind spots but also their human weakness. We all, either consciously or unconsciously, find it difficult to see truth that is not what we wish

it were. People of faith have struggled with this tendency throughout history, and we find guidance in the Bible for both justifying
and engaging in the spiritual practice of truth telling.

Consider this passage from the Book of Jeremiah:

> O LORD, you have enticed me,
>   and I was enticed;
> you have overpowered me,
>   and you have prevailed.
> I have become a laughingstock all day long;
>   everyone mocks me.
> For whenever I speak, I must cry out,
>   I must shout, "Violence and destruction!"
> For the word of the LORD has become for me
>   a reproach and derision all day long.
> If I say, "I will not mention him,
>   or speak any more in his name,"
> then within me there is something like a burning fire
>   shut up in my bones;
> I am weary with holding it in,
>   and I cannot.
> For I hear many whispering:
>   "Terror is all around!
> Denounce him! Let us denounce him!"
>   All my close friends
>   are watching for me to stumble.
>   "Perhaps he can be enticed,
>   and we can prevail against him,
>   and take our revenge on him."
> But the LORD is with me like a dread warrior;
>   therefore my persecutors will stumble,
>   and they will not prevail.
> They will be greatly shamed,
>   for they will not succeed.

Their eternal dishonor will never be forgotten.
O LORD *of hosts, you test the righteous,*
    you see the heart and the mind;
let me see your retribution upon them,
    for to you I have committed my cause.
Sing to the LORD*;*
    praise the LORD*!*
For he has delivered the life of the needy
    from the hands of evildoers.

—JEREMIAH 20:7–13

To understand Jeremiah's perspective on truth telling, some historical background will be illuminating. In this passage Jeremiah preaches about the impending destruction of Judah and its capital city, Jerusalem. The passage comes right after Jeremiah's incarceration at the hands of the temple priests.[2] The Babylonian Empire had been making inroads into Judah by manipulating and enlisting the temple priests. The priests heard Jeremiah's prophetic words, realized that Jeremiah might threaten their patrons' interests, and placed him in the stocks at the temple gate. They were trying to get Jeremiah to stop talking, an effort not without irony, since no one to whom Jeremiah preached about the mayhem believed him—everyone thought he was crazy. He was not, of course, and not long after Jeremiah's death the Babylonian Empire invaded Judah and took the people of Israel captive.

After he was released from the stocks at the temple, Jeremiah offered the lament we have here. He declared that he had gone so far as to try *not* to preach the words that God was giving him, but doing so had caused him physical pain: "[W]ithin me there is something like a burning fire shut up in my bones" (verse 9). Jeremiah did not want to preach news of impending doom in the salad days of pre-Babylonian Judah. It was a peaceful time. The people were not listening, the priests were persecuting him, and

Jeremiah would have stopped if he could have, but even his own body compelled him to tell the truth.

Now consider Jesus's words in this passage from the Gospel according to Matthew:

> [F]or nothing is covered up that will not be uncovered, and nothing secret that will not become known. What I say to you in the dark, tell in the light; and what you hear whispered, proclaim from the housetops. . . . Do not think that I have come to bring peace to the earth; I have not come to bring peace, but a sword.
>
> For I have come to set a man against his father,
> and a daughter against her mother,
> and a daughter-in-law against her mother-in-law;
> and one's foes will be members of one's own household.
>
> Whoever loves father or mother more than me is not worthy of me; and whoever loves son or daughter more than me is not worthy of me; and whoever does not take up the cross and follow me is not worthy of me. Those who find their life will lose it, and those who lose their life for my sake will find it.
>
> —MATTHEW 10:26B–28, 34–39

In this passage, much as in the text from Jeremiah, Jesus tells his followers that future suffering for them and for all the people of Israel is inevitable. He speaks of a time when households will be turned against one another and chaos will reign. Unlike Jeremiah, he makes no complaint about having to say these hard-to-hear words, but he recognizes that they will not make him or his disciples very popular. He motivates his disciples using stark language: "[W]hoever does not take up the cross and follow me is not worthy of me" (verse 38). Jesus wants to make this truth known: following him would not be easy.

Both Jeremiah and Jesus preach about an upcoming time of destruction and suffering. Each brings that message to people who do not want to hear it. Their audiences and constituents are ready to ignore difficult truths or even to persecute the one who says the things they do not like. Jeremiah and Jesus offer two different explanations for doing what they do.

Jeremiah uses the metaphor of having to get the truth out of our systems as though it were a disease; he tried to keep the truth inside, but it made him sick. Who has not had the experience of saying a hard truth and feeling better afterward? Any therapist can tell you that the hard truth we withhold will sicken us, but the hard truth spoken can be our liberation, our salvation. If the sensation of holding in the truth is like nausea, then saying a hard truth is like throwing up. It might be awful in the moment, but afterward we experience relief and healing. This is how Jeremiah makes sense of his need to find the truth.

Jesus offers a different justification for preaching hard truths by describing the kingdom of heaven, the world as God envisions it. Jesus describes the kingdom by offering four contrasts between the here-and-now and the coming day:

- That which is covered now will be revealed in the kingdom.
- That which is secret now will be made known in the kingdom.
- That which is in darkness now will be brought to light in the kingdom.
- That which is whispered now will be proclaimed in the kingdom.

Jesus offers a description of a kingdom of God where everything is known, seen, clear, and true. When we are in a place of illusion, rather than living in the midst of revealed truth, we feel numb. To offer another, and perhaps slightly less disgusting, medical illustration: choosing to live in illusion is like treating symptoms with painkillers, rather than experiencing real healing. When we take painkillers, we have relief from our pain, but nothing really changes. When we find healing, we experience transformation. When we are on painkillers, we lose the pain but also much more. When we have true healing, we are alert to everything that's happening around us. We can be reflective and can learn and grow.

Jesus tells us much about the kingdom of God in his ministry. Whether that kingdom is something we find after we die or something we can find here in this life is a question theologians have debated for centuries. But one attribute of the kingdom that Jesus lifts up in our passage from Matthew is this: In the kingdom of heaven, the truth is out. Today, Christians look to stories about the kingdom in the Gospels with a sense of mission. Jesus describes the world God envisions. In the kingdom, the poor are cared for, prisoners are visited, sins are forgiven, and children are precious. People of faith are charged with making our world more like that. This passage from Matthew teaches us that in the kingdom all is known—the good, the bad, and the ugly alike. The person of faith is thus charged with making known that which is hidden.

Jeremiah responded to the call to tell the truth, but it was hard for him. It was hard for Jesus, too, and he warns his disciples to expect this difficulty. For today's leaders, truth telling is no easier. In these two examples from Scripture, the leaders' words have little effect on the people around them. No one believed Jeremiah, and Jesus's disciples did not understand what he was trying to say. One way leaders today can avoid the pain that both Jeremiah and Jesus suffered is not to burden themselves with one-way truth telling. At least most of the time, we as leaders need not take it upon ourselves to "announce" the truth, expecting others to listen. Instead, we can work with communities in such a way that leaders and constituents seek the truth together.

Good evaluative practices are collaborative in nature: communities come together to define what success might mean and how the organization is progressing toward that ideal. Collaborative processes are less likely to leave the leader scapegoated when unpleasant truths come out, like Jeremiah in the stocks at the temple gate. Much as conflict is part of the life of ministry but should be avoided whenever possible so as not to waste energy unnecessarily,[3] one-way truth telling should be reserved for cases when speaking a hard truth "announcement style" is the leader's only option.

Evaluative practices as exercises in truth telling find theological mooring in (1) prophetic mandates to speak God's truth, and (2) faithful people's responsibility to make the world more like the kingdom of God. Therefore, insofar as holy clarity is made up in part of telling the truth, we can see that there is sufficient biblical evidence for arguing that God wants us to tell the truth, and that doing so is part of faithful living.

Clarity as Beauty

Up to this point, I have described the merits of holy clarity primarily as a means to an end: communities of faith that find clarity in their mission, purpose, and actions are more efficient in bringing about transformation in the world and in the lives of faithful people. I have argued that God calls upon us to tell the truth and that, in this way, ministers throughout history (from prophets to Jesus and his disciples) have been called upon to bring clarity more fully into the world. We must not ignore the fact that clarity is pleasing to God not only in its utility. We can find in the Bible evidence that clarity also has an aesthetic value that God appreciates and that we can learn to appreciate as well.

> *The law of the* LORD *is perfect,*
>   *reviving the soul;*
> *the decrees of the* LORD *are sure,*
>   *making wise the simple;*
> *the precepts of the* LORD *are right,*
>   *rejoicing the heart;*
> *the commandment of the* LORD *is clear,*
>   *enlightening the eyes;*

the fear of the LORD *is pure,*
     enduring for ever;
the ordinances of the LORD *are true*
     and righteous altogether.
More to be desired are they than gold,
     even much fine gold;
sweeter also than honey,
     and drippings of the honeycomb.

                                   —PSALM 19:7–10

In this passage, the psalmist writes about the law of God using the language of a love letter. He describes it as not just true and righteous, but sweet, desirable, revivifying, and leading to joy. He uses the term "clear" to describe not just the law's truth but also its elegance and beauty. This love language signals to us that holy clarity is not just something that leads us to do the right thing; it has merit unto itself in more than its utility and practicality.

When I was in college, I had a roommate with whom I shared a dorm room for three years. One night, we were up late talking about what we wanted to do with our lives. Knowing my habit of keeping a meticulously neat desk, she said, "Sarah, you should find a job where you get to organize your desk all day long." I often think of these words and smile, because as a teacher of administrative leadership for ministry, I actually spend most of my time organizing large, long-term projects, all of which have folders on my physical desk and on my computer desktop. In fact, my love for a neat desk is more than just appreciation of a good habit. Neatness and organization certainly free up time and creative energy, so that I can focus not on finding lost papers but on making progress in my work. But on another level, I do appreciate the beauty of a smooth-running system, an efficient process, a well-run conference, a carefully planned event.

In chapter 1, I noted that many ministerial leaders treat administrative tasks as a time-wasting bother. Because they do not enjoy administrative tasks, they either procrastinate (always a bad idea) or delegate (sometimes a bad idea) central ministry tasks, such as connecting with people, collaborating with teams, and maintaining efficient systems for their work. I believe that such practices are more than bad leadership for ministers. They also can be, quite literally, ugly. Some leaders, of course, take the aesthetic value of clarity too far, worshiping perfect bulletins and flawless altar flowers, becoming easily distracted from ministry or worship when one detail is out of place. That said, we must appreciate that holy clarity is more than helpful, more than useful. God is pleased when we are thoughtful and careful and attendant to the truth simply because truth is beautiful, as is God's law, which we seek to follow and to bring more fully into the world. Wanting to know the truth because the truth is worthy and lovely is sufficient justification for evaluative practices in ministry programs; ministerial leaders do not cop out when they say, "We should know the truth, because the truth is beautiful and worth knowing."

Blindness versus Sight, Both Spiritual and Physical

In some of the most familiar miracles Jesus performs in the Gospels, he heals people who are blind:

> They came to Bethsaida. Some people brought a blind man to him and begged him to touch him. He took the blind man by the hand and led him out of the village; and when he had put saliva on his eyes and laid his hands on him, he asked him, "Can you see anything?" And the man looked up and said, "I can see people, but they look like trees, walking." Then Jesus laid his hands on his eyes again; and he looked intently and his sight was restored, and he saw everything clearly.
>
> —MARK 8:22–25

Some of these miracles, like the one described above, follow the same structure as other forms of bodily healing, such as those Jesus performed with the man who was lame and the woman with the issue of blood. Others, however, blend together physical and metaphorical understandings of vision, and the person who regains sight also gains spiritual insight:

> *They brought to the Pharisees the man who had formerly been blind. Now it was a sabbath day when Jesus made the mud and opened his eyes. Then the Pharisees also began to ask him how he had received his sight. He said to them, "He put mud on my eyes. Then I washed, and now I see." Some of the Pharisees said, "This man is not from God, for he does not observe the sabbath." But others said, "How can a man who is a sinner perform such signs?" And they were divided. So they said again to the blind man, "What do you say about him? It was your eyes he opened." He said, "He is a prophet."*
> —JOHN 9:13–18

Still other miracles address not physical blindness but purely metaphorical blindness, in which people cannot "see" what is directly in front of them. Consider Luke's description of the events that took place after Jesus's death and resurrection: the risen Christ joined two disciples as they walked on the road to Emmaus. Not recognizing him (or not "seeing" him), the disciples engage this "stranger" in discussion about the recent events of Jesus's trial and crucifixion. The disciples recount to Jesus what had taken place, and he responds:

> *"Oh, how foolish you are, and how slow of heart to believe all that the prophets have declared! Was it not necessary that the Messiah should suffer these things and then enter into his glory?" Then beginning with Moses and all the prophets, he interpreted to them the things about himself in all the scriptures.*
>
> *As they came near the village to which they were going, he walked ahead as if he were going on. But they urged him strongly, saying, "Stay with us, because it is almost evening*

and the day is now nearly over." So he went in to stay with them. When he was at the table with them, he took bread, blessed and broke it, and gave it to them. Then their eyes were opened, and they recognized him; and he vanished from their sight. They said to each other, "Were not our hearts burning within us while he was talking to us on the road, while he was opening the scriptures to us?"

—LUKE 24:25B–32

In passages like this one we find that the Gospels treat physical sight and spiritual sight as though they were at least related, if not one and the same. Those who can see physically can also see the truth of Jesus's divinity. Those who are "blind" to Jesus's presence are given the ability both to recognize who he is (physically) and to know that he is the Christ (spiritually) at the same moment. Seeing and knowing are used interchangeably. Furthermore, Jesus speaks using images related to physical vision to describe the human condition:

Do not judge, so that you may not be judged. For with the judgment you make you will be judged, and the measure you give will be the measure you get. Why do you see the speck in your neighbor's eye, but do not notice the log in your own eye? Or how can you say to your neighbor, "Let me take the speck out of your eye," while the log is in your own eye? You hypocrite, first take the log out of your own eye, and then you will see clearly to take the speck out of your neighbor's eye.

—MATTHEW 7:1–5

Jesus could have described any part of the body in the image he uses here. Why did he not say, "You see the sliver in your neighbor's finger, but not the stake in your own arm"? He uses the activity of seeing and the capacity for vision to describe spiritual knowing. We must first be able to "see" ourselves in all our frailty before "seeing" and judging another person. Sight and knowledge have everything to do with one another in the Gospels.

There is no better way to describe the relationship between this seeing-and-knowing and holy clarity than to explore the life and ministry of the apostle Paul. Paul himself experienced a miracle that combined spiritual and physical blindness at his conversion. When he served the temple priests, persecuting Christians and living under the name "Saul," Paul was blinded by a bright light before Jesus spoke to him, telling him to enter the city of Damascus to await instructions about what he was to do. His temporary blindness persisted after the vision ended, however, leaving Paul in need of assistance.

> *For three days he was without sight, and neither ate nor drank. Now there was a disciple in Damascus named Ananias. The Lord said to him in a vision, "Ananias." He answered, "Here I am, Lord." The Lord said to him, "Get up and go to the street called Straight, and at the house of Judas look for a man of Tarsus named Saul. At this moment he is praying, and he has seen in a vision a man named Ananias come in and lay his hands on him so that he might regain his sight." But Ananias answered, "Lord, I have heard from many about this man, how much evil he has done to your saints in Jerusalem; and here he has authority from the chief priests to bind all who invoke your name." But the Lord said to him, "Go, for he is an instrument whom I have chosen to bring my name before Gentiles and kings and before the people of Israel; I myself will show him how much he must suffer for the sake of my name." So Ananias went and entered the house. He laid his hands on Saul and said, "Brother Saul, the Lord Jesus, who appeared to you on your way here, has sent me so that you may regain your sight and be filled with the Holy Spirit." And immediately something like scales fell from his eyes, and his sight was*

restored. Then he got up and was baptized, and after taking some food, he regained his strength.

—ACTS 9:9–19

Paul went directly from blindness to belief when his sight was restored at his conversion. The transformation that took place in him during his brief experience of blindness was not unlike that of a caterpillar inside a cocoon. When Ananias arbitrated his sight's restoration, Paul was able to see not just his surroundings, but the truth of Christ's divinity and the awful reality of his previous evil ways. Paul went on, in his ministry, continually to clarify the meaning of the Christian faith and the nature of the community that would live out that faith through the church. Seeing and believing remained a powerful metaphor for him throughout his ministry, and even with his sight restored he was painfully aware of the incompleteness of human knowledge. In his letter to the Corinthians he writes:

Love never ends. But as for prophecies, they will come to an end; as for tongues, they will cease; as for knowledge, it will come to an end. For we know only in part, and we prophesy only in part; but when the complete comes, the partial will come to an end. When I was a child, I spoke like a child, I thought like a child, I reasoned like a child; when I became an adult, I put an end to childish ways. For now we see in a mirror, dimly, but then we will see face to face. Now I know only in part; then I will know fully, even as I have been fully known. And now faith, hope, and love abide, these three; and the greatest of these is love.

—1 CORINTHIANS 13:8–13

Paul recognizes that human knowledge is never complete, and human vision is never completely clear (as though "in a mirror, dimly"). But he believes that to strive after more perfect clarity is a worthy task for a Christian and for the body of Christ, the church.

Ministerial leaders can work with their communities to find joy in that striving as well.

A church in New England celebrated a 300th anniversary a decade ago. On its 250th, in the 1940s, leaders at the church had put together and placed a time capsule in the church sanctuary to be opened on the 300th. Unfortunately, no one thought at that time to make a map showing the capsule's location. Therefore, although lore had passed around the church that the time capsule was there, somewhere, no one knew exactly where. As the anniversary celebration grew closer, the church leaders of the 1990s became desperate. Where was the capsule? A member with a metal detector, having heard that the capsule was in a steel box, came to the church and began hunting. In his exploration, he discovered a surprise—not the time capsule, but a strange fact about the church's architecture. Large pillars in the sanctuary, which members had assumed to be weight-bearing, turned out to be hollow. Leaders had talked for years about how hard it was even to consider expanding the sanctuary with these huge pillars blocking so many congregants' views. Although to this day the time capsule has not been found, the sanctuary has changed completely. The pillars were knocked down, the seating was expanded, and a whole new atmosphere for worship has been created.

Sometimes it is hard for ministerial leaders to motivate a religious organization's stakeholders to go hunting for information and truth. One way to encourage them is to remind them of the wonderful possibilities that lie in wait for those who once were blind and now can see. Blindness, both physical and spiritual, limits us and keeps us from seeing both hard truths and promising possibilities. By describing to members of a faith community the biblical basis for appreciating sight—both the literal and metaphorical varieties—participants can grow more excited about the possibilities that await them if they open their eyes.

Holy Clarity and the Role of the Leader

I talked recently with a pastor in Boston who was once a seminary professor. We were discussing my school's master of divinity curriculum, in particular what a student needs to learn in seminary to be effective in ministry. He contended that students must study the Bible intensively while in theological school, for even on their first day in ordained ministry, they need to know more about the Bible than those in the congregation do.

Whether we agree with this logic or not, it is safe to say that it is unfair, even inappropriate, to expect an ordained minister to know more on the first day about the *faith community* she or he is called to serve than those in the congregation do. Ministers who arrive in new settings with "all the answers" about where the church needs to go tend to struggle. It takes time to get to know a community and to learn enough about it to articulate, in collaboration with others, its vision. That said, faith communities usually expect their pastors to have a special ability to see the organization with holy clarity. Is this a fair assumption, or is it dangerous?

In the Bible we find evidence that questions about leaders' special (or not-so-special) access to truth, clarity, and sight are far from new. In Numbers, we read:

> *While they were at Hazeroth, Miriam and Aaron spoke against Moses because of the Cushite woman whom he had married (for he had indeed married a Cushite woman); and they said, "Has the LORD spoken only through Moses? Has he not spoken through us also?" And the LORD heard it. Now the man Moses was very humble, more so than anyone else on the face of the earth. Suddenly the LORD said to Moses, Aaron, and Miriam, "Come out, you three, to the tent of meeting." So the three of them came out. Then the LORD came down in a pillar of cloud, and stood at the entrance of the tent, and called Aaron and Miriam; and they both came forward. And he said, "Hear my words:*

When there are prophets among you,
I the LORD *make myself known to them in visions;*
  I speak to them in dreams.
Not so with my servant Moses;
  he is entrusted with all my house.
With him I speak face to face—clearly, not in riddles;
  and he beholds the form of the LORD.

Why then were you not afraid to speak against my servant Moses?"

—NUMBERS 12:1–8

We read in this passage that God usually communicates enigmatically to prophets but uncharacteristically communicates in an especially clear way with Moses, expecting Moses's followers to hear his words as God's own. Today some look to their pastor with the same deference, as though their pastor's words came from God directly. Others see their pastor as having one voice and one vote, like any other member of the community. Where a faith community finds itself on the continuum between these two extremes depends largely on the theology of ordination within the faith tradition, and it also varies from person to person and from pastor to pastor.

One illustration of the confusion some faith communities demonstrate related to the pastor's special or not-so-special knowledge comes from my own experience as an ordained person who works in education. Because my vocation is in schools, but my calling is to the ministry, I have spent much of my career working in a ministerial capacity during the week but then sitting as a church member in the pews on Sundays. I have learned, now in four different church settings, how important it is for me to remain neutral on governance matters except in cases where I feel unusually strongly about an issue. I must be careful not to undermine the pastor, as my ordained status torques whatever I say. I use the term "torque" rather than "weight" because I do not believe my ministerial vocation necessarily increases the respect others give me. Rather, especially in settings where ministers in the pews are rare, I get the feeling that fellow church members do not know quite what to do with me! I have been a member of one church where there were literally a dozen ministers who were also members; in that setting, I did not feel that I received undue deference. In another setting, I felt that it was impossible to participate in church leadership because my words were too often taken as gospel, when I was simply trying to participate in conversation. Different communities vary in their understanding of the loftiness or normalcy of ordination. Effective ministerial leaders must be able to "read" this deference and understand it for what it is. Failing to interpret this climate of deference accurately can lead to confusion when communities work together toward holy clarity.

The community's understanding of the pastor's special or not-so-special access to holy clarity about the organization's status and mission must play a role in how the pastor encourages widespread participation in evaluative practices. Some communities respond to evaluation processes saying, "Whatever the pastor thinks is best is fine with me." In other settings, participants say, "This will give us a chance to evaluate the pastor's work; let's have a closed meeting to talk about it." Both these extremes have their pitfalls; the wise pastor anticipates them and teaches the congregation about collaborative forms of learning.

Even in churches with the flattest of hierarchies (such as in congregational polity structures, where the pastor is a member of the congregation), the pastor plays a special role in leading the community to find clarity. First, pastors have theological training that enables them to help others make spiritual sense[4] of the world around them. Second, for the most part pastors spend more time physically and mentally present in the organization than many lay leaders do, in that lay leaders often have full-time commitments outside the church, whereas ministry is the primary occupation of many pastors. Third, many believe that ordained ministers have a special calling and a mystical connection with God and God's will, which they cultivate through regular prayer so that God might guide the religious organization's work.

For many pastors, insofar as their traditions permit them, it is best to strike a balance between the extremes described here. They need to help those who place their pastor's knowledge on a pedestal to understand that laypeople too have wisdom to share about the state of affairs in the faith community. They must show those who see the pastor as one-among-equals that the pastor has training, insight, and authority that give him or her a unique ability to guide the community toward holy clarity. Whether the faith community sees this as the pastor's God-given duty or simply as part of the pastor's job description, no one benefits when the pastor abdicates her or his leadership role in motivating the community to learn about itself. In the Bible we see that God has, throughout history, chosen to use people to serve different functions, even those like Ananias, who have no idea why they have been chosen. The pastor who can embrace this role as head clarifier, without becoming arrogant about having special access to God's will, is best able to serve in this capacity.

Earlier in this chapter I said that it is easiest to describe holy clarity by contrasting it with unclarity; we know clarity when we see it, and we know murkiness when it is all around us. A religious organization that has achieved holy clarity is one in which participants and leaders have a good sense of what they are called to do, how their programs are going, what the programs' effects have been, and where growth areas lie. Evaluative practices that have, in part, been borrowed from the secular world can assist a community as it discovers these realities. Even if borrowed from secular organizations, evaluative practices can be traced back to biblical teachings. These roots show the person of faith the appropriateness of evaluative practices not just to the community's material success but to its spiritual relevance.

It pleases God to see a faith community that is striving to know and to learn and to understand more and more about its calling, mission, impact, and effectiveness. At the same time, in this life and in this fallen creation, our knowledge will never be perfect; through a mirror dimly is often the best we can do. We must work at striving toward holy clarity, all the time. The next chapter describes specific steps ministerial leaders can take to make this clarity a reality.

Case Study: Wherever to Start?

Alex always thought during seminary that he would like campus ministry, so he was delighted when he received a call to serve an Evangelical Lutheran Church in America chaplaincy at the state university near the liberal arts college he had attended.

Perhaps it was because he was so close to college age himself, but he just couldn't picture himself in a parish setting, ministering to the elderly on one end of the spectrum and Sunday-school kids on the other. He had loved college and had experienced his first sense of calling to ordained ministry while lying on the Quad one night, looking up at the stars and asking God for a sign of where he could be of most service. The feeling of security that came over him when it first occurred to him, right then and there, to go to seminary had never left him. He was excited now to help others who were seeking God's guidance.

The problem was this: he had no idea what he was supposed to be doing all day. When he began his appointment in August, he thought that the silence in the campus center, where he shared an office with all other approved campus ministers, was due only to the fact that students were not around. But nothing really changed in September. The office was still silent, even though all the other administrators and the students he saw in the building seemed frantically busy. His board of directors, all Lutheran laypeople except for one local pastor, met only quarterly. They had met once with Alex since he was called to the post, and the only time he was invited to participate was for one agenda item titled "minister's report." It came after the reports from the chair, treasurer, and endowment chair, and Alex honestly had nothing at all to say in that first meeting. He had met hardly any students and was mostly feeling overwhelmed with loneliness, even boredom.

He had sent out e-mails to all students who had indicated on their incoming student forms that they identified as Lutheran, but only one student had written him back; she then failed to show up for a lunch meeting they had scheduled. Alex pored over old meeting minutes to learn more about what his predecessor had done with her time; all he could find were bullet-point board reports where she had indicated a "ministry of presence" philosophy of campus ministry.

Alex had no workspace of his own, so his books from seminary were still in boxes in his new apartment, where he was beginning to spend more and more time. Whenever he went to unpack them, the spines stared back at him: Luther, Augustine, Bultmann, Day. When would he ever have the chance to use these theologians in his work, if he did not have any students to teach, a community in which to preach, or a congregation to lead? Would it perhaps have been better to serve a congregation after all?

Discussion Questions

- Have you ever taken a new position as Alex did, where you were unsure of your role? What was that like?
- What are some first steps Alex can take as he crafts a role for himself in this setting?
- How might concepts related to holy clarity help Alex understand his position and perhaps even connect some of his seminary learning with his current situation?

Chapter 3

~

Getting Leaders Thinking
Finding and Fostering Clarity

IN HER BOOK ABOUT THE PEDAGOGY OF LEADER-
ship guru Ronald Heifetz, Sharon Daloz Parks provides what one
might call a new, or at least unconventional, definition of leadership: "[T]he function of leadership is to mobilize people—groups,
organizations, societies—to address their toughest problems. Effective leadership addresses problems that require people to move
from a familiar but inadequate equilibrium—through disequilibrium—to a more adequate equilibrium."[1] The form of leadership
Daloz Parks describes depends on a leader's ability, as described
in chapter 1, to work with groups of stakeholders to face facts. We
can begin to see, through definitions of leadership like these, why
evaluation literature has begun to describe evaluation as an act of
leadership. Here are just a few examples of ways in which evaluation is an act of leadership, not just reporting.

Susie Quern Pratt, an evaluation consultant who has for many
years helped program directors working with foundation grants to
design effective evaluation strategies,[2] teaches program directors
(and those who help them) to place learning at the heart of their
evaluation practices. She encourages grantees to see improvement
in their organization's effectiveness as the primary goal, and accountability to funders as an important but secondary goal.

In her book on evaluation for ministry programs, Jill Hudson
writes that the main purpose of evaluation is to foster growth in

organizations and their leaders. "Twenty-first century evaluation is not about looking at shortcomings and failures but rather about learning from them and planning for the next step."[3] Hudson argues throughout her book *When Better Isn't Enough: Evaluation Tools for the 21st Century* that faulty motivations (such as displeasure with a pastor[4]) pervade many congregational evaluation processes, while the only constructive goal of evaluation must be learning and, ultimately, improvement.

In their book *Level Best: How Small and Grassroots Nonprofits Can Tackle Evaluation and Talk Results*, Marcia Festen and Marianne Philbin consistently seek to disabuse their readers of the notion that evaluation is all about bean counting after a program is in place. "Think of evaluation as a tool designed to help you understand your organizational strengths," they suggest, "and to throw some light on areas in need of improvement."[5] As we consider these three evaluation "experts," we see a theme upon which they seem to agree: evaluation, when done well, equips leaders to do a better job in that it gives them the information they need to lead an organization toward growth and improvement. Evaluation practices give leaders the tools they need to make evidence-driven decisions and to help constituents face important issues.

As they read these examples, however, leaders may have a sinking feeling. Even leaders who realize and accept that evaluation is an important leadership practice sometimes become insecure in the face of evaluation, worried that even as they appreciate its importance, they simply do not know how to do it. Chapter 1 provided some perspective on why evaluation is more important in today's postmodern religious context than it might have been in modernity. Chapter 2 pointed out overlap between the evidence-driven thinking associated with evaluation and the theological principles associated with holy clarity. But now a leader reading this book might be wondering, "Where even to start?" Often a leader's first reaction, upon hearing about the central importance of evaluation to leadership, is to feel overwhelmed, unprepared, or even resentful.[6]

I offered some evaluation consulting to a highly competent colleague who serves an educational organization. She reported that she needed help because evaluation was the one area in her leadership role that left her feeling genuinely out of her depth. Her feelings seemed associated with an assumption that evaluation is unusually complicated as leadership tasks are concerned. In some settings, evaluation is treated as a sophisticated science accessible only to experts. My colleague felt as though she had missed some top-secret training day on how to conduct evaluations that everyone else in the religious professional world had attended. I have worked hard to communicate to her again and again, *Evaluation is not rocket science; any leader can do it. But it does require a different way of thinking about our work, and that way of thinking starts coming to us naturally only with practice.*

Therefore, in this chapter, I present four evaluation practices that I hope will get leaders and their teams started with evaluation. When used both in private discernment and public conversation, they can guide leaders and their stakeholders into this new, evaluation-oriented way of thinking. Once they get started, leaders will see that one size does not fit all and that all evaluation practices must be adapted to an organization's needs. That said, by getting started, leaders in religious organizations can get past their overwhelmed "I-don't-know-where-to-start" inertia. The tools also provide a shared language, so that groups of leaders can challenge one another to grow in their capacity to evaluate their organizations. Once that mentality—both individually and collectively—sets in, fear of evaluation recedes, and organizations begin to face facts together.

Four Evaluation Practices That Work

Leaders in religious organizations can use the following four practices in two ways. First, they can doodle them on the backs of napkins at coffee shops to clear their own heads and to make sense of the dynamics of their organizations. All good leaders spend time thinking about their organizations and considering both how they are limited and how they can grow. Disciplining that daydreaming with the perspective provided by evaluative tools is a useful practice for leaders who seek clarity. Second, leaders can use the tools as conversation starters with groups of stakeholders, so that leaders and their partners can find holy clarity together. Alone or with a group, they are meant to provide simple starting points that spur evaluative thinking.

The Condition/Intervention Diagram

Kathleen Cahalan writes that any project or program in a religious organization responds to a set of conditions.[7] Therefore, it is useful for leaders, both on their own and in working with stakeholders, to articulate (1) to what condition their program is responding and (2) how their program is the appropriate response that will bring about change in that condition.

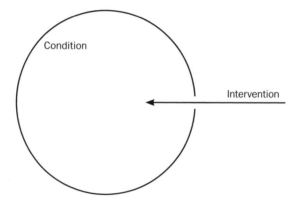

Using this condition/intervention (C/I) diagram is simple. First, name the "condition" that the organization cares about. Then describe the "intervention" or "program" designed to bring about a change in the condition. One condition can have numerous intervention arrows leading into it, but the diagram has most utility when, at first, leaders consider interventions one at a time. A condition might be described this way: "The children in our congregation need to be fully included in the community while also receiving special, age-appropriate attention that suits their spiritual-formation needs." An intervention then might be called "Program for Children and Youth," with subheadings "Sunday School," "Confirmation Program," and "Youth Group."

At first glance, this exercise may seem too obvious to be an evaluation exercise, but so often ministry programs function for years without ministry leaders' expressing the condition that led to their creation and that justifies their continuation. I created the C/I diagram while in conversation with a leader whom I was helping to write a grant report. She had listed the various activities the grant had supported, but that list lacked an animating principle that could describe to her grantors why these programs were important and bringing about positive change. What was missing in the report was a clear sense of what held these programs together: To what condition were all of them responding? Once the leader was able to articulate the condition, the programs' cohesion became apparent.

There are three ways that a C/I diagram can help a leader both to think like an evaluator and to lead a community to face important realities. First, the diagram lays bare an organization's concerns, using plain and simple language. Leaders cannot evaluate their organization's progress without clearly articulating the organization's goals and reasons for existing. By breaking apart the condition and the intervention, the leader can communicate more effectively: "This (condition) is the situation we care about, and this (intervention) is what we're doing to make a difference."

Second, the diagram shows an organization its own blind spots about the condition it seeks to change and the appropriate interventions. Sometimes the connection between the intervention and the condition for evaluation is not sufficient to be useful, and the diagram can uncover this sort of disconnect. Festen and Philbin write that every organization has a theory of change[8] that underlies its choices. That theory is an unspoken assumption that *if* the organization takes a particular action, *then* a particular change will result. Building on the previous example, a theory of change might read, "If we have a strong program for children and youth, children and youth will feel included in our congregation and grow in faith." When leaders use the C/I diagram, their theory of change comes to light.

Leaders might, through the condition/intervention diagram, discover leaps of logic within their theories for change. For example, they might be using an *intervention* like a program for children and youth to address the *condition* of church-membership decline. The theory of change would then read, "If we have a strong program for children and youth, more people will join our church." The flaws in that theory of change leap to the eye, for between the condition and the intervention, too much is taken for granted. This theory of change assumes that families in the community are seeking church homes, that the program for children and youth will generate good publicity beyond the church, or that an inadequate children-and-youth program was in part responsible for decline in the first place. Discovering these gaps in the organization's theory of change ensures that evaluation will be logical. If the condition and the intervention were not sufficiently related at the start, how can we expect that the intervention will bring about a change in the condition? Can we truly evaluate a program's effectiveness if its logic was flawed from the start?

Third, the condition/intervention diagram prepares leaders to engage in the two forms of program evaluation: process evaluation and outcomes evaluation.[9] Process evaluation focuses on the intervention itself: What went well? What went poorly? What might we do differently next time? Outcomes evaluation focuses on changes in the condition that come as a result of the intervention: Has there been a noticeable and measurable change in the condition that caused us to launch the intervention in the first place? Both process and outcomes evaluation are important in religious organizations today, but many leaders focus nearly all of their assessment energy on process evaluation.

I direct the field education program at the seminary I serve. Through that program, all master of divinity students complete a one-year, part-time internship in a "teaching parish" that has special training to work with students. When I first took over leadership of the program, I read about the training events through which teaching-parish leaders were prepared to work with students. The evaluations participants completed were stellar. Lay leaders who attended the workshop described having learned a great deal and feeling prepared to welcome their student in the fall; they loved their time on campus and often expressed interest in returning for the next training session.

During a comprehensive assessment process in my first year, however, I encountered a different reality, one in which students routinely reported, "My teaching-parish committee has no idea what it's doing." From these conflicting stories, it became clear to me that our *process* was excellent, but our *outcomes* needed some work. I used the written evaluations participants had completed to learn what it was that lay leaders had liked so much about the training—for why throw out the baby with the bathwater?—but then looked to students to tell us what was missing from their experiences, so that we could improve the outcomes. Since then, we have made some changes to the training day and have added a monthly newsletter in the hope that, over time, students will begin reporting to us that their congregations were truly prepared to work with them. By no means could I ignore the process evaluations, for when working with volunteers, leaders always must care about providing participants with positive experiences that will bring them back for more. That said, when the outcome is disappointing, the whole purpose for having a program (to address a condition) gets lost. Process evaluation without outcomes evaluation fails to address the fundamental need that justified the program's creation and supports its continuation.

This example serves to illustrate that religious leaders cannot ignore process evaluations, even in the face of disappointing outcomes. The quality and integrity of their interventions do matter, as their outcomes will never be reached without interventions of high quality. That said, both processes and outcomes need to be evaluated, even though—let's face it—process evaluations are far easier to conduct. Although it is simpler to hand people surveys at the end of an intervention, asking them whether they have enjoyed their experience, than it is to monitor elusive change in a condition, it truly is the change in the condition that matters most. A church with the most organized and entertaining Sunday school in the world might not be successful in including children in the life of the church. A church with a poorly managed Sunday school can still cause a child to feel that he is part of the community. The condition/intervention diagram provides leaders with an exercise through which they can articulate what they care about and what they are trying to accomplish, uncover the logic underlying the actions they have chosen to take, and prepare to evaluate both their own actions and the changes those actions bring about. A simple circle with an arrow can serve as a tool a leader can use to create clarity that energizes and galvanizes a community.

Logic Models

Many evaluation professionals rely on different forms of "logic models" for organizing their work. A logic model lays out what needs to happen for their organizations to meet their goals, fully taking into account the many factors that lead to a hoped-for change in a condition.

RESOURCES	INPUTS	OUTPUTS	IMPACT	INDICATORS
What does the organization need to invest by way of money, staff, time, and partnerships for this program to be successful?	What do leaders have to provide— events, courses, resource centers, hotlines—to make the program happen?	What needs to result from the provision of these resources in order for the program to bring about the hoped-for effect?	What change takes place in participants as a result of this program?	How would someone know that these results took place? What would be the measurable, visible, discernible signs that the desired impact resulted from the program?

Leaders use logic models by "backing in" from the right-hand column indicators. First, leaders consider what change they would like to see take place in a condition as a result of a program. I usually recommend that leaders engage a group in considering the question, "If our program did everything it hoped to do, what would success look like five years into the future?"[10] Once group members have described some outward, visible signs they would take as an indication that the program was fulfilling its purpose, leaders then ask, "If that is the change we hope to see, what would need to have happened first?" That is when attention turns to the Impact column. Leaders repeat that same question, "If that is the change we hope to see, what would need to have happened first?" as they move all the way back into the Resources column. Here is an example of a logic model that I used when my family was deciding whether to get a pet. (Please note: I use this example not to trivialize the practice of creating a logic model, but rather in an attempt to render the exercise accessible.)

RESOURCES	INPUTS	OUTPUTS	IMPACT	INDICATORS
Pet supply stores that carry food, toys, scratching posts A local veterinarian Money to buy supplies Time and attention to devote to the cat Feelings of affection toward animals	We adopt a cat We provide the cat with what she needs to be healthy We pay attention to the cat and give her love	We have a healthy, well-adjusted cat who is loved	We love our cat Our daughter learns to be kind to animals . . . or get scratched! We have more joy in the house	We are all a bit more cheerful and playful Our daughter is nice to our cat and to other animals she meets We can trade "that darned cat" story with friends and neighbors We refer to our cat as a member of the family

Much like the condition/intervention diagram, logic models show leaders the importance of linking their investments in a program and the change they hope will come as a result. Often there is no logical connection between the indicators (what success means) and the resources invested in a program; church leaders or members expect a huge turnaround without devoting resources to a program. In other cases, they invest the wrong sorts of resources—when, for example, leaders authorize the purchase of expensive equipment without considering the personnel training needed to use that equipment. Through working from right to left when using logic models, leaders begin to see how important it is to start by articulating the attributes of success and working from there, rather than rolling out "inputs" or program initiatives without considering the impact they are meant to have.

Logic models were developed with the support of the Kellogg Foundation, which still provides resources for using them.[11] Someone who has used them before might have looked at my tables here and said, "No, no, no, that's the outcomes column, not the impact column." I tend to resist "scientification" of exercises like logic modeling, however. I believe all leaders need to adapt these exercises, using language that makes sense to them, and that we waste energy when we argue over semantics with instruments that are meant to provide clarity rather than create more complexity. The point of using a logic model is to think a program all the way through, from the resources that need to go into it to the change leaders hope will come out of it. Logic models help us appreciate how much thought has to go into a ministry program and how seamless the internal logic of a program must be for the desired impact to be realized. The "indicators" column also sets us up to begin the process of an evaluation, and I return to that concept later in this chapter.

Stakeholder Mapping

While C/I diagrams serve to answer the question "What are we trying to do?" and logic models ask "How are we trying to do it?" stakeholder maps answer the question "Who cares?" Often leaders in religious organizations take for granted that they know who is affected by their work. Either the most obvious, or the loudest, individuals are taken into consideration when leaders wonder whom to include in their planning and evaluation processes, but key participants are forgotten because of inattention to the many ways that programs touch people's lives. Stakeholder maps lift up the many individuals who are influenced by even small organizations. Those individuals cannot be forgotten by religious leaders as they reflect on their work and its impact.

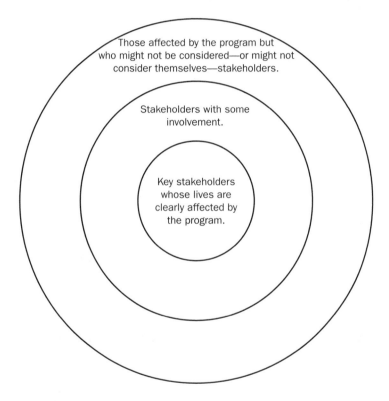

I developed stakeholder mapping as an evaluation practice after "doodling" one during a conversation with the key leaders of a religious organization at a large university. I feared that the leaders were giving far too much attention to the "usual suspects"— students, staff, and faculty who attended every one of their events and made up their leadership team. As they were thinking about evaluation, they were doing little to learn from students who went to program events only occasionally, faculty members who perhaps participated in one or two retreats, or staff members who only read about their programming in the campus newspaper. All those members of the community had something to say about the program; it was just not a huge part of their lives. I drew the "dartboard" image in that conversation to encourage the leaders to think not just of the "bull's-eye" types who would participate even if the programs were not very interesting, but to consider even those in the outermost circles who perhaps only heard about their programs secondhand.

Leaders can use stakeholder mapping by considering the question "Who has a reason to care about our organization?" In the margins of the stakeholder map, they can generate a list of those whose lives have been changed, even if only in a limited way, by the organization's ministry. Then the leaders consider which stakeholders are central to the organization's activity and very much influenced by it. Whose lives among those stakeholders are affected only somewhat or not at all? By the term "stakeholder," I mean those whose lives are changed, influenced, or affected to varying degrees by a program. Some stakeholders are central and find the program in question to be of deep importance in their lives. Others care about the religious organization but are not involved on a day-to-day basis. Different sorts of stakeholders are part of every organization, and when the time comes to make decisions about the organization, those who are affected at various levels must be taken into consideration by leaders.

By mapping stakeholders, leaders begin to see a number of attributes of their programs more clearly. They notice who in their wider community is only tangentially affected but perhaps should be affected more by the religious organization's work. They see connections among stakeholders they might not have recognized previously. For example, after I began using stakeholder mapping more intentionally, I facilitated a stakeholder mapping exercise with a leadership team at a Christian university. One member of the team suggested that the university's trustees should be on the list. Another suggested that members of the organization's community-relations committee—a large group of concerned citizens in the town beyond campus—were stakeholders. As we moved trustees to the outermost circle, and the visiting committee to the innermost circle, the program director suddenly realized: one member of the visiting committee was a trustee! This recognition led to animated discussion about how that committee member might be able to connect the organization with the university's trustees. These kinds of crossovers in the stakeholder map show leaders the breadth of their program's impact and remind them not to forget constituents as they evaluate the program or plan to make changes.

Data Collection Strategy

Whether a leader is trying to create a process for monitoring the effectiveness of an intervention or a group of leaders is seeking to conduct a comprehensive evaluation, data collection must take place if leaders are to take advantage of the wisdom of their gut feelings and then take those insights a step further into real evidence. We begin to look toward data, or evidence, to answer our questions only after we have identified these questions:

- What is happening and what ought to change (C/I diagram)?
- How, step by step, might that change take place (logic model)?
- Who will be affected and who can give us insight (stakeholder map)?

Once we are confident that we can answer those questions, we know where to search for data that can demonstrate the effects of our organization's activities.

Why so much fuss before we collect data? Why can we not simply send out a survey, pull together a focus group, or interview some participants? As any statistician can tell you, data collection and analysis processes are only as good as the questions with which they start. The best evaluations are focused, with particular questions in mind *for appropriate groups of people.* To focus an evaluation, Cahalan says, leaders must identify the subject and purpose of the evaluation, the audiences the evaluation seeks to inform, key evaluation questions, and someone to lead the process.[12] Even if leaders are not engaged in a formal evaluation process, they must refrain from collecting data first and framing questions second. They must first identify what they want to see happen, how they hope to make it happen, and who will be affected; the exercises leading up to this exploration of data or evidence collection and analysis prevent leaders from rushing into data-gathering mode.

DATA SOURCES	COLLECTION METHODS	ANALYSIS STRATEGY
Individuals who can share information	Interviews	Qualitative: "Coding" and reporting
	Focus groups	
Participation records	Surveys	Quantitative: Calculating
Existing documents	Observation	
	Website hits counter	

Building on Cahalan's proposal that organizations must deliberately plan an evaluation strategy, I make use of data-collection strategies that lay out who can help inform leaders about the organization's impact, how information might make its way from those who can provide evidence to leaders, and what leaders might do with that information once they have it.

Data sources most commonly take the form of people:

- participants deeply and not-so-deeply involved,
- members of the community where the organization functions who might not think of themselves as stakeholders but

who still might be touched by a program or have a reason to care about it, and of course,

- leaders.

It is important that all sorts of affected people are taken into consideration when leaders ask themselves who can provide them with information; otherwise, it is likely that the most concerned participants—for better or worse—are the only ones included in evaluating or monitoring an organization's effectiveness.

Of course, people are more than data sources. They are involved in the program's creation and evaluation at every phase. The reason we consider various groups of stakeholders at the data-collection phase with a particular level of care is that it is easy, when beginning an evaluation, to mistakenly assume that the program's leaders are automatically the only people who need to be involved in telling the story of the program. The discipline of considering people's insights carefully at this phase helps leaders avoid the natural blind spot that comes with overfamiliarity with a program and a related neglect of numerous voices.

Collection methods should be determined only when leaders know what it is they seek to understand better; the common adage for researchers is "Let the question drive the method." Ideally, whenever possible, leaders should build data collection into what they were going to be doing anyway;[13] that is what is meant by "existing documents" in figure 3.5. For example, if members of a religious education committee wish to understand the impact of a confirmation program, and confirmands write statements of faith at the end of the course, those statements might be a useful data source for answering the question at hand. When no existing documents are appropriate for answering a particular question, a leader can make use of written surveys, interviews (one-on-one conversations), focus groups (larger-group, cross-fertilizing conversations), and participation rates.

Before collecting data, however, leaders should take the time to decide what they will do with the information once they have it.[14] In that sense, the *analysis strategy* should be in place before leaders engage the stakeholders in data collection. This approach is important for several reasons. First, researchers are often warned not to "go fishing in the data," perusing data and pulling out of it quotations or numbers that support what the leader wants to hear. A clear analysis strategy put in place before data come in prevents leaders from fishing, and prompts them to analyze the data as objectively as possible. Second, data collection on a leader's part always sends a signal to a community. Leaders should be warned not to collect data that they do not expect to use, or to which they do not plan to pay attention. When stakeholders are asked what they think about something, they expect not only that they will be heard, but also that change might come as a result. Leaders should take care to consider the signals their questions might be sending and the possibility that they will ratchet up expectations of change or improvement in a program.

I have a pastor colleague who recently took a position in a large congregation. He put a survey in the church bulletin, asking for input into his sermon topics. He limited the survey by listing topics upon which he hoped to preach at some point and used the data he received to help him prioritize when he would address which theme. Had he not heeded the input he received or ignored the suggestions altogether, he would have set the congregation up for disillusionment. This is one way that research and evaluation differ: researchers worry less about how the questions they ask might shape a community's expectations, whereas leaders in religious organizations must take care to avoid collecting data in a way that sets up a community for disappointment. A rule of thumb: if you cannot change it, take great care in how you ask about it.

The data we gather are either quantitative or qualitative. We analyze data quantitatively when they come in the form of numbers. Most typically, we enter those numbers into some form of statistical-analysis software (Excel, SPSS) to learn about trends (increases and decreases) and correlations (relationships between different trends). Qualitative data come to us in the form of words, either spoken or written. Most evaluation in smaller religious organizations (like most churches) takes this form—because, first, quantitative studies usually require a large number of participants (some say at least thirty; some say much more than that) if they are to tell a leader anything valid. Second, religious experience is not easily quantified, but people are often able to describe what they think of a religious organization's activity. Qualitative data are most commonly analyzed through a process of "coding," in which either written surveys, or transcripts of interviews or focus groups, are analyzed, with the researcher looking for particular themes. Each theme is given a code, and text is sorted according to those codes. Some software is available to sort large data sets, but colored highlighters are often sufficient for analyzing qualitative data in a smaller religious organization.

The data-collection strategy is a means whereby leaders can move from hunch-driven leadership to evidence-driven decision making. It provides a methodical, disciplined approach for staying in touch with stakeholders—not just the squeaky wheels, but all whose lives are touched by a religious organization's work—without either misleading them or misinterpreting the experiences they share. When used in conjunction with the other three evaluation techniques described in this chapter, different kinds of data collection can combine to further a simple but comprehensive evaluation strategy.

Four Evaluation Strategies at Work Together

Throughout this section, I have built one evaluation practice upon another to demonstrate how a leader can use simple evaluation techniques to clarify the purpose, activities, and effectiveness of a religious program. The following diagram explicitly lays out how the four can systematically work together toward a comprehensive evaluation strategy that can either be implemented in a deliberate process or used to monitor an organization in an ongoing way.

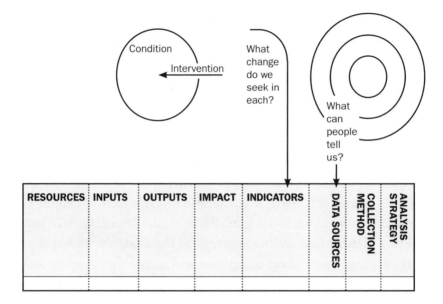

We begin the process at the top-left corner with the condition/
intervention diagram. In that diagram, we name the concern we
hope to address and the program meant to bring about change in
the condition. A visible, measurable change in the condition can
be "dropped into" the logic model as an "indicator" of an "outcome." The intervention itself is an "input," and a participant's activity in the intervention is an "output." By using logic models in
conjunction with the condition/intervention diagram, we can be
sure to remember as leaders that our true hope is a change in the
condition; we maintain a clear vision as leaders when that is in the
foreground of our daily work.

Logic models can be fused with data-collection strategies to
ensure that indicators are quickly connected to data sources for
measurement.[15] One of the most common mistakes leaders make
in evaluating programs is that they measure "outputs" (how many
people participated, who took part, *what happened*?) rather than
"indicators"—*what changed* in those who participated and in the

community where the program took place? When we fuse logic models with data-collection strategies, it is important that we first consider who can provide the most useful information about the indicators we seek. It is here that stakeholder maps come in; they prevent leaders from overreliance on "the usual suspects" to show them whether the hoped-for change is taking place, disciplining them to consider more broadly who might have insights into indicators.

As leaders move in and out of these four practices, they ideally begin to adopt a new way of thinking about their work. They become more deliberate about what they do, take less for granted, say no with more confidence to tasks that do not further their missions, and say yes more readily to learning more about the effects of their activities. Leaders also start to adapt these back-of-the-envelope exercises to their own learning needs and styles, a response that is to be commended and expected. Again, evaluation is not rocket science. Evaluation is a practice in which all leaders engage every day. The only question that remains is, Will we do it well or poorly? Deliberately or accidentally? Will we trust our hunches or generate reasonably objective data? Will we see clearly what our organization is doing and what it is up against, or will we allow the murkiness of a complex time to overwhelm us? If we start small, with "doable" evaluative practices, we might discover that evaluation is not just one more task on a list but a helpful practice that makes us better at everything we do.

The Leader's Role in Implementing Practices

As I stated earlier, leaders can use practices like the four described in this chapter on two levels. First, they can use them in their own reflection on what their organization is doing and then present their findings in different ways to different constituencies to check their assumptions and spur conversation. In this sense, the four practices are tools for thinking and communicating about the organization's activities and vision. Second, leaders can use them to lead an evaluation, methodically planning a process and engaging stakeholders in a comprehensive assessment. Ideally, leaders engage in both sorts of evaluative practices at different times. They might deliberately conduct an evaluation one year, with the assistance of an internal coordinator or even an external consultant, but then go on to use evaluative practices to address one or two questions a year. Festen and Philbin write, "For smaller organizations, we recommend tackling only a couple of questions at a time and evaluating on a rolling basis."[16] Even when not engaged in a formal evaluation process, evaluative ways of thinking and communicating can encourage an organization's leaders and stakeholders continually to ask themselves important questions about what they are doing and why.

This said, clarity can come at a cost. Evaluative practices often uncover the uncomfortable truth that some of a ministry's programs are not working. Almost without fail, an evaluative process that includes stakeholders who have not previously been asked their impressions turns up information about people who are unhappy with the organization. One reason leaders in religious organizations avoid evaluative practices is that they are either afraid to hear negative information, nervous that the information they gather will suggest changes that they do not have the energy or resources to make, or fearful that programs found to be ineffective will be cut without a second chance, causing grief to themselves or others. Just as even the best teachers have one or two students who do not appreciate each course, no ministry program that includes more than a handful of people can please everybody all the time. How can a leader be prepared for the fear, nervousness, and grief (anticipatory or otherwise) that accompany evaluative practices like the ones described here?

Leaders must anticipate that some fear and related conflict will surround evaluation processes. Strategies for minimizing damage from those conflicts include transparency and isomorphism.

When leaders are "transparent," they are as aboveboard as possible about the evaluation process in which they are involved. Because it is good evaluation practice to think through whom to include, what questions to ask, and what will be done with data before a single survey is sent out, it should be easy for leaders to communicate transparently about what an evaluation is meant to accomplish. And yet it is not in most cases, for evaluation is not just an activity but a way of thinking, and many constituents in religious organizations do not understand why it is necessary or why learning and improvement are the ideal goals. Because those who do not understand the importance of evaluation are likely to resist it, leaders must be "aggressively transparent," educating their constituents and the organization's stakeholders at every phase of evaluation. With every interaction between leaders and stakeholders during an evaluation process, constituents should be informed why the evaluation is taking place, what will change (or be subject to change, or definitely not change) as a result of the evaluation, and what will happen with the words and other data participants share.

Even when a leader works hard to maintain transparency in evaluative practices, stakeholders often feel suspicious of possible ulterior motives when they hear the term "evaluation." Leaders should anticipate what faulty assumptions stakeholders might make, and clear them up ahead of time. For instance, if leaders believe that a comprehensive program evaluation of the church might be misunderstood as a referendum on the pastor's effectiveness, they should state up-front that this is not the case. Many a pastor has been burned by a "churchwide evaluation" that was actually not churchwide at all, but was rather a performance review of the pastor cloaked in a comprehensive evaluation. It is for this reason that I recommend focused evaluations that center on one "intervention" at a time, such as an evaluation of an adult Bible study rather than an entire Christian education program, as it is too easy in a catchall process to single out one person. One intervention should be selected, and at every opportunity leaders should state transparently exactly why and how they are evaluating this intervention. For instance, if adult Bible study attendance has dropped precipitously, leaders could describe the evaluation by saying, "We realize that the Bible study remains important to several members in the congregation, so we wish to understand why attendance has decreased and how we might meet the needs of more members interested in adult Christian education."

Second, leaders can engage in practices that foster in stakeholders a trust that, although an evaluation process might lead to some change, the change will be counterweighted by respect for tradition and history. Scott Cormode, in his book *Making Spiritual Sense*, writes, "If a leader knows that she is going to have to do something controversial or disruptive, she can find another place to emphasize unity."[17] To continue with the example from the previous paragraph, if leaders were to determine that they should move the adult Bible study onto the Internet, they might take such simple steps as using the same font style in the online Bible study that had been used for the in-person Bible study's handouts. This familiar "look" would draw links between the "old" Bible study and the new in ways that would help those who enjoyed the old style to feel welcome. Cormode also recommends that leaders rely on pre-legitimated processes when engaging a community in doing something new.[18] As I said in chapter 2, the Christian tradition—particularly in the Bible—has always honored and respected the practice of telling the truth and finding clarity. Leaders must teach communities that evaluation can simply be part and parcel of life in a religious organization. At first, stakeholders might not accept this assumption. At those times, leaders are wise to disguise evaluative practices in the "clothing" of other activities in which the organization engages. For example, if an organization's members are not accustomed to surveys but they gather for discussion about their organization's effectiveness at their annual meeting, the meeting can be turned into a focus group without that term ever being used. The less new-fangled evaluation seems to be, the safer participants will feel, and the less they will fear that an evaluation's findings might be used in a threatening way.

This said, sometimes the threats that come from an evaluation process are quite real; "sunsetting" ministry programs is part of the work of a leader, and some believe it ought to happen more. Often religious organizations float along for years with ineffective programs. They fail to ask themselves key questions about why organizations exist and how their activities relate to their concerns. Their resources, inputs, outputs, and hoped-for impacts do not relate logically to the changes they hope to bring about. They lose touch with stakeholders and fail to gather information beyond anecdotal reports. Because they neglected to maintain clarity consistently in their work, some religious organizations' evaluation processes may indeed uncover the need for significant change. As Daloz Parks writes, they need to travel "from a familiar but inadequate equilibrium—through disequilibrium—to a more adequate equilibrium."[19] By no means is this a simple or easy process, but tools like the ones described in this chapter can be used in many ways, through creative adaptation based on a community's needs. When used in a context-appropriate manner, these exercises help communities move toward greater clarity and, ultimately, a stronger sense of purpose.

Case Study: The Bait-and-Switch Task Force

Sandy is the director of human resources for a pharmaceutical branch office in a suburban area and a member of Holy Family Church, a Roman Catholic congregation with strong lay leadership and a beloved priest, Father Tom. After she had been a member for about four years, Father Tom invited her to participate in a task force that he said would be working to discern a vision for the future, especially related to the church's family ministries. He told her that the parish council[20] had commissioned this task force, and that members of that council had been particularly keen on her being a part of it. Sandy was flattered by the invitation, particularly because, as a single person, she felt that Holy Family was her family. In the back of her mind she had occasionally wondered whether her unmarried status caused her to be viewed as a second-class citizen by other parishioners. Any concern she had that she could not participate in the life of the church as a single person was at first allayed by this invitation, and Sandy embraced the new role.

Sandy learned two things at the first meeting of the task force that quelled her early enthusiasm. First, she discovered that one reason the parish council had commissioned the task force was related to a human-resources problem: The religious education lay staff member's position was about to be cut from the budget without any plan in place to carry that ministry forward after her departure. To compound the damage, the staff member, Julie, had not yet been informed of this imminent change.

Second, the convener of the task force, Al, seemed to have quite an ax to grind. Al had been a member of Holy Family for more than thirty years and had, with his recently deceased wife, raised four children in the congregation. His feeling that the family ministries in the church were the most important function it served became abundantly clear in the first meeting. Al, who had served in the military early in his life, worked at a desk job in a manufacturing company. He used warlike language when describing societal threats to Catholic families and children in general, and he began the meeting with a long speech during which he pounded the table. Sandy understood this to be Al's style, as well as a sign of his lingering grief, but she also worried that his anger on that first day would bring an adversarial tone to all conversations.

Much of the conversation on the first night the task force met sounded like anger-edged whining. Why were there no cuts to the music ministry but dramatic cuts to religious education? Was this just the bishop's way of getting rid of Julie, a strong female leader whom the kids loved? Sandy perceived quickly that the priest had invited her, with her human-resources expertise, to provide a voice of calm reason to a difficult situation. But she also felt used; at first she had thought that perhaps she had been invited to give a single person a voice in the family ministries of the church. Now it just seemed that she was assumed to be available to provide free consulting on HR. After the meeting, she wrote and saved, without sending, two e-mails:

Dear Task Force Colleagues:

Thank you for including me in our energetic discussion last night. As we move forward, I wonder if we might take some time to review our mandate and consider how to share the purpose of our work with the parish council and the congregation. I for one would benefit from some clarification of our role and tasks, so I might pray and discern in between our meetings. Any ideas?—Sandy

Dear Father Tom:

Thank you for inviting me to participate in the visioning task force you have convened. Unfortunately, because of other commitments, I am unable to continue on the task force at this time. See you Sunday!—Sandy

Sandy went to bed, not having decided which e-mail to send.

Discussion Questions

- What do you think about this task force having been assembled at all?
- How might Father Tom have approached the matter with Sandy in a way that her good feeling might not have dissipated?
- How might Sandy play a constructive role, were she to continue on the task force?

Chapter 4

~

Planning and Restructuring Programs
Bringing in the Light

IN CHAPTER 3, I FOCUSED ON THE WAYS EVALUATION can help a leader in a religious organization to create clarity where once there was murkiness. In this chapter, I turn my attention to new program creation. If you are not getting ready to create a new program in your ministry setting, it might cross your mind to skip this chapter, but to do so would be to misunderstand how program creation works.

In all organizations, and Christian organizations in particular because they so often span generations, programs are in a constant state of flux. They begin; they are sustained; they plateau and decline and die. Birth, maturation, death, and rebirth are happening under the surface, even in cases where a program appears to be stable and unflagging. Program creation happens far less frequently than internal program reinvention, when leaders build upon and revise traditional, continuous programs from within. But the principles of invention and reinvention are similar enough to study them together here. In this chapter I describe some of the theory that leaders can use to create or recreate a program. Then I suggest how to build evaluation into a program in such a way that the initial clarity in a new or renewed program can be sustained through ongoing evaluative practices.

Writing and Rewriting Ministry Programs

When I first began writing sermons, I used a laborious and time-intensive technique that I called "reverse outlining." I would study the Bible passages appointed for the day, pray about them and research them, and then start writing without an outline. I would let my thoughts run wild, and through that practice I would feel the Holy Spirit working with me to apply the text to a life of faith. After my Jack Kerouac–style, stream-of-consciousness rant, I would read what I had written and then write an outline. When I rewrote the sermon, using more structure but without losing the Spirit's muse, a message would emerge that was more easily communicated than the first, free-form draft. Today, I no longer use this process in a formal manner. Instead, I read the passages on which I will be preaching well in advance and allow them to percolate in my mind. By the time I sit down to write, or to prepare mentally for a sermon without a manuscript, I have thought a message all the way through.

Program planning in religious organizations often takes the same form: first musing, then structuring, then musing some more. We try new strategies for ministry and outreach, give new ideas a chance, and experiment with ways to connect with people. Then we consider what has happened and create an "outline" of sorts in the form of a program plan that can be communicated to others and sustained over time. Through reflective practice in the midst of ministry, programs take shape in such a way that ideas can be anchored in the culture of an institution. Rare is the occasion when a group of leaders sits down to brainstorm to create a new program. Although one hears occasionally of ministerial leaders who create numerous programs, most create altogether new programs only rarely, as even larger institutions seldom have the space, energy, or resources to launch more than one or two new programs a year. But leaders often reflect together on what is happening within an existing program and how its stream-of-consciousness beginnings can be given intentional contours and thus a more robust life.

In short, ministerial leaders tend more often to build upon and strengthen programs that are already up and running than to create new programs. A junior-high youth group emerges from a gaggle of sixth graders playing air hockey after church. A men's fellowship grows out of an annual fishing trip. A food pantry morphs into a soup kitchen. It is leaders' responsibility to create infrastructures that uphold such initiatives and that anchor programs in the life of a community, connecting them to the resources they will need to sustain life beyond the happenstance and haphazard phase. The theoretical resources that have been most helpful to me in midcourse, "reverse outlining" processes, whereby a free-flowing activity becomes a structured program offering, have come from the world of institutional change theory. The more we understand about change as leaders, the better equipped we are to guide the change toward fulfilling our organization's mission as effectively and faithfully as possible.

Some people might question my belief that program planning theory and institutional change theory are one and the same. I once served as an outside evaluator for one of the Lilly Endowment-supported Programs for the Theological Exploration of Vocation (PTEV). The leader of the PTEV initiative to whom I reported, knowing that I was a doctoral student at the time, asked me about my dissertation topic. I told her that I was going to write about institutional change in campus religious life, and that I was using the PTEV as a case study.[1] She asked some polite questions, and we moved on with the evaluation process. Several months later, I saw the program director in another setting, and she said that she had been thinking differently about her work with the PTEV since I described it as a case study on institutional change. She had thought of the PTEV as a program, not a change initiative, but over time she had begun to realize that new programs do bring about institutional change, as their very existence has a catalytic effect on the community around them.

I argued in chapter 3 that models for program planning can be used both for new program creation and for strengthening and renewing continuing programs. Ministerial leaders often rely as much on the Holy Spirit as they do on a strategic plan. In even more cases, they rely on intuition and gut feelings when putting a new program on the ground. Leaders have a hunch that there is a need to reach out to a population, to serve a community, or to try something new. So they make a foray into new territory to give something a try. If that foray goes well, they must backtrack to answer crucial questions about leadership, resources, and sustainability. Program planning models can help them do this, just as they help in the creation of new initiatives or the re-creation of lapsed initiatives. Strengthening and renewing programs are continuous activities that leaders must consider even when working on stable and effective programs. Even programs that appear to be working well "on their own" cannot continue over time without effort, intentionality, and structure.

New programs in a community—even a historic community like a long-established church or university—are like teabags in a cup of hot water. Over time, they change the color and nature of their setting, even if just a little. Change leadership theory can help a person responsible for leading or creating a program to consider what must go into such a program and the institutional change it will, by nature, create.

Two Theories of Change

In this section, I describe two change-theory models that a leader in a religious organization can use to foster greater clarity. Much like the models presented in chapter 3, these two theories can help a leader brainstorm privately about how a program is moving along or can help a group of leaders better understand their work and the challenges they face. Generally, change theorists favor lists: step-by-step models of how institutional change moves or should move. On one hand, some criticize these lists as an oversimplification of dynamic processes in organizations and warn that lists should be used to stoke thinking but not as a basis for developing a plan.[2] On the other hand, even the most adamant purveyors of lists offer up-front caveats that the steps are never quite as simple as one might hope. Much like the stages of grief, stages of change loop back onto one another, smash into each other, and are sometimes skipped altogether.

In fact, one could argue that the similarity between stages of grief and stages of change, in the way they are lived out, is due partly to the fact that grief accompanies change. Whenever an individual or a community enters a time of change, there are both real losses and ungrounded fears of loss. Furthermore, the line between the real and the imagined losses is always unclear. The hope is that, through honesty on the part of leaders—or "transparency," as described in chapter 3—and careful planning, the loss or fear of loss that comes from change might be tempered by the excitement that accompanies opportunities to renew organizations, strengthen them for the long term, and increase their impact.

Kotter's Steps in Leading Change

Harvard Business School's John Kotter proposes eight steps toward program planning in an institutional setting by starting with eight common mistakes that cause an initiative to fail:

1. Allowing too much complacency.[3]
2. Failing to create a sufficiently influential guiding coalition.[4]
3. Underestimating the importance of a shared vision.[5]
4. Radically undercommunicating the vision.[6]
5. Permitting a very small group to block change toward the shared vision.[7]
6. Failing to show participants encouraging signs of success early.[8]
7. Resting on laurels too quickly.[9]
8. Neglecting to anchor changes in the organization's structure and culture.[10]

From these "what not to do" warnings, Kotter derives his eight steps toward the creation of a program or change initiative that is bound to succeed:

1. Establishing a sense of urgency.
2. Creating the guiding coalition.
3. Developing a vision and strategy.
4. Communicating the change vision.
5. Empowering broad-based action.
6. Generating short-term wins.
7. Consolidating gains and producing more change.
8. Anchoring new approaches in the culture.[11]

I first encountered Kotter's eight steps just after taking up service as a campus minister at a large state university. Few programs were in place in the ministry center when I began my work, as participation had declined to nearly nothing; high turnover in the ministry, among chaplaincy staff and students, had interrupted momentum. Although I did not use Kotter's eight phases as a road map, following them in exact sequence, they became a helpful rubric for me. I took them as advice and used them as diagnostic tools for recognizing where opportunities had been missed and might be recaptured in the future. Each of Kotter's steps has something special to say to a leader in a religious organization, but there are three in particular I wish to highlight here: urgency, communication of the change vision, and short-term wins. I choose these because, in my experience, they are the steps religious organizations skip most frequently, at the peril of their programs' success.

First, urgency: I once heard that a pastor telling a church to change when it sees no reason to do so is like a doctor prescribing chemotherapy to someone who comes in complaining of a headache. A ministerial leader who urges change without first helping participants to see why change is necessary is bound to fail. Conversely, to frighten participants into willingness to change is both unethical and manipulative. It is common in religious organizations for leaders to cry wolf, scaring stakeholders with "the sky is falling" warnings to promote a particular agenda. Leaders might, without ill intent, frighten each other and parishioners with dramatic presentations on declines in membership or giving. Yet I have never heard of a church membership drive that succeeded when the motivation of those doing the evangelism was fear. Finding the right level of urgency is an art in leadership.

Second, communicating the change vision: We all know that participants in religious organizations tend to be busy people. Those who choose to be part of religious communities are often "joiners" who participate in numerous other communities, such as schools, neighborhoods, political groups, and close-knit families. Although this is not always true, it is true often enough that leaders must consider how to communicate change to overstimulated people. In each faith community of which I have been a part, there is an inner circle of participants who read everything they receive from the religious organization, studying it and responding to it. In the case of many change initiatives in religious organizations, communications are designed for the deeply involved and overconscientious. The very involved are precious members of faith communities, but communications about change should not aim for them. They should aim toward the middle—the attention span and engagement of the typical person, rather than the especially invested member. Most of us need to read or hear about something a few times before it is completely clear to us or before we remember it well. If we communicate clearly and often, the very attentive participants in the faith community may be puzzled by the frequency, but the word will get out. For instance, imagine that a Christian college has decided to fulfill its sense of mission by relocating from a wealthy suburb to a struggling urban setting. The what, how, and why of that decision might start to sound like a broken record to attentive faculty, but repetition of the message through every medium or to every constituency will ensure that few tangentially involved supporters will be left in the dark. Alumni, community members, and the parents of students might attend only one event or read only one newsletter, so information about the move had best be there, or these groups will be missed altogether.

Third, generating quick wins: Change tends to move slowly in religious organizations. When change happens slowly, it is hard to see. Think of the proverbial activity of "watching grass grow." Leaders need to be mindful that the energy that moves a change effort ahead comes from enthusiastic participants who want to see change; if those participants cannot see change, energy is bound to flag. Kotter suggests that leaders must build in short-term successes that make a visible splash in order to keep energy for change running high.

The president of the state university campus I served as a chaplain[12] was such a believer in the power of short-term wins that she authorized an official committee called "Quick Wins." I served as a member of that committee. Our only function was to hear suggestions from members of the campus community about inexpensive, easy, and quick changes that the university could make that would improve the life of the school. For example, one faculty member suggested that each course catalogue should list its relevant academic year not just on the front of the book, but on its spine, so that older catalogues lined up on a shelf could be distinguished from one another. Even though adding those words to the spine of a publication required practically no money or effort, the faculty member felt heard, the publication improved in its usefulness to faculty, and a visible sign of change emerged. Leaders in religious organizations cannot always bring about change quickly, but they can create outward signs of hope and progress, reminding the community that change is happening, and that change can be good, so that old patterns do not set in while the grass is growing.

Kotter's eight steps of leading change provide a shared vocabulary for leaders in religious organizations, but they must be adapted to specific settings. Many authors concerned with institutional change have provided similar phase-oriented descriptions of how change happens in organizations. The one I provide next has emerged from my work with religious organizations, particularly church-related educational settings. But even these must be tailored to different types of religious organizations that make meaning in different ways.

VELMA

The five phases of change I have developed to describe best practices in program planning for religious organizations bear obvious similarities to Kotter's eight steps. The ways the steps I have proposed diverge from Kotter's relate to some special considerations with which faith communities are likely to be concerned and to which leaders in religious organizations must attend with particular care. The steps in program planning I posit are:

- *Vision*: Leaders work together to create a shared mental picture of what a new program might do and how the community in which it is situated might be changed because of it.
- *Empower*: Leaders consider whom they can charge with responsibility to move that vision ahead. At this phase, it is crucial to select leaders who are qualified and ready to carry forth the vision, a group much like Kotter's "guiding coalition."
- *Learn*: Those leading the initiative must, fairly quickly, ask and find answers to these questions: (1) What have other institutions done that can inform this change initiative? (2) What theoretical resources can help us as we move ahead? (3) What do we need to learn about our own context before moving forward?[13]

- *Make a foray*: Make informed decisions and carry them out, beginning with a pilot program that has careful assessment built into it, and continuing into the life of the new program.
- *Anchor*: As with Kotter's model, it is important for leaders to think ahead about monitoring and strengthening the program after it is on the ground.

The acronym that comes out of these steps is "VELMA," which I like because, as a slightly out-of-fashion, grandmotherly name, the term VELMA can be introduced to groups without sounding stuffy, imitative of corporate practices, or officious. A group that is either planning a new program or studying how to change an existing program can do a VELMA exercise. A group of leaders can brainstorm what it would take for a visionary program to empower leaders, support learning for those leaders, move the organization forward toward important decisions, and anchor the program into the culture of the institution by monitoring and supporting it beyond its inception.

I developed this model for a course I taught in 2006 on technology and ministry, and since then I have taught it to students in my course on program planning and evaluation. In that latter course, students are required to design feasible ministry programs, with a particular context in mind. Although students are permitted to use either Kotter's steps or the ones proposed here, nearly all of them used VELMA. Although I believe that it is possible for religious leaders to borrow heavily from secular writings in finding guidance for their work, churches and other faith-related organizations are special and different in some ways, and leaders must take these differences seriously if they wish to borrow from the secular, business world. VELMA takes these differences into account.

Both Kotter's model and VELMA propose that program planning and change leadership begin with a "visioning process." I once interviewed the leader of a major initiative at a Christian college who was given a significant grant to create a new campus ministry program in her setting. She said that she first needed to work with colleagues, talking with them about their hopes until they could "picture [the program] alive."[14] Only then—when they had a shared mental picture of what they were aiming for—could they begin planning. This is a literal but truthful way to describe a visioning process: talking with each other until all can see the program alive in their minds' eyes.

The nature of visioning in religious organization has a special urgency, however. In faith-related institutions such as churches, participants might hold a variety of images about the true mission of the organization. In a business setting, one can assume that all hope the business will be profitable. In a religious organization, however, some might see a successful ministry program as one that brings in new disciples, while others want to take better care of current members. Some might see individual spirituality as most important, while others believe that communal togetherness is the ideal. In such a context, where it is not uncommon to find a pew of ten people, no two of whom agree on what the organization is truly "for," talking and thinking about vision are crucial.

Furthermore, many participants in religious organizations grapple with the very term "vision" when that vision comes from human beings. They may argue, for instance, that ministerial leaders should not have a vision of their own, but should rather look to God for vision. When I hear that line of argument against "visioning" by leaders and participants in religious organizations, I argue that all of us are interpreters of God's will. We might have varying ideas as to what God expects from our ministry settings, but none of us has perfect insight into God's vision. In a faith community, I believe that no one person can cast a vision but that the leader can do a great deal to set the tone. He or she can bring a vision of something that has worked in another setting or a strong idea of what an organization ought to be doing, but even a leader with a well-formed sense of vision must work collaboratively within a faith community to discern what God's will might be.

Again in the case of empowerment, both Kotter's model and VELMA lift this practice up as an important one, but the contours of empowerment in a religious organization take on a shape different from that in the secular world. In the for-profit world, managers empower workers to help them become more productive, and therefore more profitable. Although productivity among workers is important in nonprofit and religious organizations, the "bottom line" is not a product but a transformation. Both leaders and participants are part of that transformational experience, and no person is treated simply as a means to an end. That said, religious organizations are famous—or, one might argue, notorious—for providing leadership opportunities for people who might not have the chance to lead outside the church. One hears stories of men who are janitors during the week but deacons at church, men who find in their church an opportunity to live out a calling that their work life cannot provide. One also hears, however, of people being placed in church leadership roles for which they are not ready or qualified.[15] Furthermore, as volunteerism declines in some settings, religious organizations are often ready to give leadership roles to anyone who will take them. It is not possible to empower leaders toward the creation and implementation of a change without taking into consideration how important it is to get the "right people."

Leaders in religious organizations should consider these two principles when preparing to empower participating leaders for a program initiative's guiding coalition:

First, as difficult as it can be, religious leaders need to prevent people who are unwell or radically unqualified to lead from being placed in positions where those unfit leaders can hurt themselves or the institution or community itself. We all know of churches where the trustees would never permit the youth group to paint a room in the church, insisting that only a professional can do a good enough job, while at the same time selecting a chairperson for the trustee board who is untrained or even mentally unstable. As Kotter writes, choosing unprepared leaders to take the helm of a change initiative sends a message to community members that they need not take the new or renewed program seriously.[16]

Second, leaders must be ready to meet potential guiding coalition members where they are. All organizations struggle to find sufficient numbers of trained volunteers to take leadership roles, as people's lives are full and hectic. The best way leaders can recruit participants for a guiding coalition is to package volunteer opportunities carefully. They must delimit the expectations placed upon those they are recruiting and empowering to lead the charge toward change, clearly specifying the tasks to which those they recruit are committing themselves and when that responsibility will end. Leaders must make sure that the work they are empowering guiding coalition recruits to take on is meaningful and gives them both freeing limits and creative flexibility. When asked how they managed to recruit excellent leaders to further their institutional turnaround, two pastors[17] who visited my class on program planning and evaluation shared this mantra they use in their empowerment efforts: "People have time. They just don't have time to waste."

In nearly every new program initiative or renewal effort in a religious organization, the first project for the guiding coalition needs to be learning. This learning should focus on three areas: (1) the program's history and context, (2) what other organizations are doing, and (3) foundational theory to guide the effort.[18] For example, imagine a church located close to a new state-of-the-art assisted-living community. A coalition, initiated by the pastor or deacons, might come together to consider ways of reaching out to that community. As a first activity, members of the coalition can take time to learn more about the assisted-living center, assess the church's history of reaching out to seniors, and read a book together about ministry with the elderly.

Why is this learning process especially important in a religious organization? The reasons are numerous. *First*, volunteers in religious communities tend to overestimate the completeness of their understanding or insight when it comes to their religious organization and its surrounding community. For example, I once served a church located in a part of a city that was known to have a growing and active lesbian, gay, bisexual, and transgender community. As a newcomer to the city, I noticed and heard about this population right away, but when I brought the topic up, lifelong members of the church insisted that they had never heard of this community's strong presence in the area. Their overfamiliarity with the setting, compounded by their memories of different times, made it hard for them to see realities right in front of them. By taking a disciplined approach to learning, a guiding coalition can become more deeply informed and can overcome its normal blind spots.

Second, I believe that many who participate in faith communities of various kinds have an unusually deep appreciation for tradition. Leaders and guiding coalitions that appear to have a cavalier attitude toward change, in situations where traditions might be swept away without being fully understood, find it difficult to earn the trust of community members. Leaders must take the time to learn the origins of their communities' faith traditions, so that core values represented by those traditions are respected, even if the practices of the traditions themselves are set aside. Learning need not slow a change process; if a coalition divides up the tasks associated with learning and sets forth a timetable for gathering information, change can move ahead both briskly and thoughtfully.

Third, many faith communities are facing challenges different from those they have experienced in the past. As religious organizations create new programs in a quickly changing society, they often find themselves off-script, trying out new ideas with no frame of reference for how to proceed. By learning what they can, guiding coalitions can be as grounded as possible in entering new terrain, bonded by a shared vocabulary that emerged from a careful learning process.

Once the guiding coalition believes it knows what direction it should go, it must make a move. Ideally, learning leads to planning and program design, but coalition members must not get stuck in their heads. Leaders must both make a splash and begin an experiment. Over the past few years I have become an advocate for pilot programs. Because new and renewed programs are so often sailing in uncharted waters, I believe that a low-stakes first try is essential to a change process. Kotter argues that quick wins build confidence that change is possible.[19] I believe that in addition to fostering the confidence and visibility that come with an early success or attempt at success, making a first foray is important for loosening the bonds of inertia. Many religious organizations endure long periods when little changes. Stasis sets in, and change becomes unfamiliar to the point of being vaguely frightening. By making a move, a leader and her or his coalition can shake people out of their comfort zones and prepare them to embrace a new way. Furthermore, if they begin the process by making a move fairly quickly, guiding coalitions do not run as much risk of talking themselves in circles or out of any meaningful change.

Anchoring a change in the culture of a religious organization begins as the program itself is designed. Even with a first foray, the best way to start anchoring is to think about ongoing monitoring and evaluation for the short-, mid-, and long-term future of the program. By thinking about evaluation before a program is even on the ground or before an existing program has undergone any noticeable change, a guiding coalition is less likely to put a program into operation only to abandon it by expecting it to function on its own. The process of designing evaluation into the program structure helps leaders think about what kinds of stages the program might move through, and therefore what kinds of support the program will need over time. It is all too easy for leaders who expend a great deal of energy on program design to withdraw once the program has been launched, expecting someone else to handle matters from there. Designing ongoing evaluation reminds leaders that they cannot assume that someone else will magically carry the program forward. Furthermore, if evaluation activities are built in from the start, the program is less likely to fail or to become static again, as evaluation leads to virtually constant program renewal and responsive change.

Building Evaluation into a New or Renewed Program

I wrote earlier that visioning processes require leaders and participants in religious organizations to talk with one another until they can picture a program alive. With a new program initiative, they must dream together about what the program might look, feel, and sound like when it comes into existence. With a continuing program, leaders and participants talk together about what the program could be with time, energy, and resources dedicated to moving it a new direction or toward continual improvement. These discussions about vision are not just the first step in developing a new or renewed program. They are also the first steps in program evaluation.

One exercise I have adapted and used with a variety of constituencies asks program leaders and participants to articulate what they would consider to be "Signs of Success":[20]

> *Think ahead five years. Looking out across the landscape of church-related colleges and universities, what would be happening that would convince you that your PTEV initiative had succeeded in achieving its goals? (Here just take a moment to think large and dream big.)*
>
> *Now focus on your school in five years:*
>
> - *What single change would you most hope to see in the programming or pedagogical approach at your institution?*
> - *What single change would you most hope to see in the culture of your institution?*

Now focus on your faculty in five years:

- *What single change would you most hope to see in the attitudes or behaviors of individual faculty members?*

Now focus on students in your institution ten years from now:

- *What single change would you most hope to see in the knowledge, skills, behaviors, or actions of your students?*

Other constituencies to inquire about might include partner institutions, campus ministries, college alumni, and the like.

When I have used variations of this exercise in different settings, the first reaction I see in most leaders is puzzlement. How could this daydreaming exercise lead us toward assessment, which is all about data and measurement and testing? I respond that they can never know how to measure success if they are not able to articulate what success would mean in their context. Assessment requires a benchmark against which to measure progress.

Therefore, when creating a new program or renewing a continuing program, leaders must describe what success would look like. They then must talk together, early and often, about how they will know whether that vision of success is coming to life. Because it is easy to forget to ask these questions during a program planning process, I encourage leaders to ask themselves continually while designing their programs, "How will I know?" How will I know if we are meeting our goals? How will I know if we are making the right kind of progress? When leaders are mentally in "planning mode," they focus a great deal of their energy on the programs they are planning and what successful programming demands. Yet the program's success is not meant to stand only on whether participants enjoyed it. Rather, the program is meant to bring about transformation in the lives of individuals and communities. How will we know if this is happening, especially if our attention is consumed by making the program function?

This question brings us back to a topic from the previous chapter: the difference between process evaluation and outcomes evaluation. Leaders in religious organizations must consider process and outcomes simultaneously. If the process associated with a program—the lived experience of a program initiative—goes poorly, the program will fail to attract or retain participants. Therefore, leaders must care about the process. But if participants attend entertaining programs but experience no growth or transformation, the process might be excellent, but the outcome will not live up to its goals. During program planning, leaders must work together to build in both process evaluation and outcomes evaluation. That means they must have a mental, and eventually written, idea about both what a successful initiative might be and do, and what kinds of transformation they would like to encourage.

Consider this example: As a campus minister, I spent more than half of my time planning and implementing ministry programs for students, faculty, and staff at the university I served. There were certain things I knew I must provide to attract students to a program: food (of course!), other students, something fun to do. Yet many sorts of activities offer those three benefits to students. I could have hosted a keg party and covered all three of those bases. But as a campus minister, I had worked with my board to articulate a goal that we would provide students with opportunities to grow in faith, to be exposed to church life in our city, and to discern their faith and vocation. So when I evaluated our effectiveness as a campus-ministry setting, I needed to think on two levels. We will know that our process is good because students keep on coming. But how will we know if they are growing in faith, connecting with churches, and discerning their callings? To discern these transformational outcomes required more effort.

Even though conducting process evaluation is actually much easier than doing outcomes evaluation, as I have described it in this example, leaders in religious organizations often direct almost all their evaluation energies toward process evaluation. They send out surveys and conduct focus groups that raise questions related only to how the participant experienced the program, not to how she or he has changed. In other words, they focus their efforts on hearing more about how they are doing as leaders in the organization, rather than how their constituents are changing, both in the context of the organization and in the rest of their lives.

Because the natural physics of organizations is likely to skew time and energy toward process over outcomes, leaders must correct for this skewing during the design process. They must work hard to articulate what success would mean and create systems for measuring outcomes over time. By building evaluation into the program infrastructure itself, leaders can anticipate the busyness that might eventually steer them toward more of a process-oriented approach and away from desired outcomes down the line.

There are four rationales for why a leader in a religious organization must ultimately care more about outcomes than process. *First*, ministerial leaders must practice good stewardship of the institutions with which they have been entrusted. Cahalan writes, "Stewards care for organizations by keeping alive the fundamental reason that defines why an organization exists and why it embarks on the work it does."[21] The leader of a religious organization must take care not to misuse power, to waste resources, or to mistreat people or the earth. But the leader must also protect the mission of the organization, never forgetting its core purposes. Focusing on outcomes rather than processes helps leaders to care effectively for that core purpose.

Second, leaders must attend to outcomes out of respect for excellence. In their book about the character of excellence in Christian ministry, theological education scholars Greg Jones and Kevin Armstrong write:

> *Excellence in Christian ministry is perceptible and palpable. Yet it requires a capacity for measuring life by the complexity of judgment and grace as well as the more standard measures of "bodies, budgets, and buildings." . . . How do we calculate the effect of reconciling forgiveness, the value of a deepened*

prayer life, the impact of passing on faith to a child, the quiet presence of sitting with a dying parishioner or hammering nails to help provide housing for a homeless family? Such activities are crucial to the way of discipleship, yet they often seem less significant when measured against the ways of the world.[22]

The ways excellence in ministry is measured differ from the ways we measure the effectiveness of a particular program. Running the program might take up much of our time, but our hopes for the program are lofty if we seek to promote an excellent way of life. Therefore, success is in the excellence of the outcome, not in the program that led to it, and we therefore must direct our evaluative energies toward those outcomes.

A *third* rationale for emphasizing outcomes relates to the very thesis of this book: Clarity is an inherently valuable quality toward which leaders should strive. When leaders are able to articulate the transformation toward which they are working, they motivate others to seek that goal too and thus bring in more support. I argue that this clarity also strikes people as moving, beautiful, and inspiring. People love to hear clear communication, and when a leader can say what she or he seeks to accomplish at the deepest levels, she or he earns constituents' trust.

A *final* rationale relates to the natural life cycle of ministry programs. All life is cyclical in some way, and as I noted earlier, even historic ministry programs wax and wane over time. If leaders are focused mostly or exclusively on program offerings rather than on the goal toward which those programs strive, they can easily get stuck. The program offering becomes distanced from its original goal and stops achieving that goal, and then the program outlives its purpose. If leaders put purpose first, they are free to change program offerings as time and circumstance dictate. Over time, different means are required to meet the same goal. Leaders who put the programs' goals first do not get too attached to particular means for reaching those goals.

Consider this example: In the field education program I lead, ministers who supervise students play a central role in the students' education. Program leaders have always dedicated a great deal of attention to supporting supervisors, requiring them to take a course during their first year working with students and then subsequent continuing education. A few years ago, as part of a comprehensive assessment, our leadership team studied why continuing, experienced supervisors were reporting mixed experiences—some truly loving continuing education and some dreading it. What we learned was that supervisors (1) still wanted to be together, and (2) still valued continuing growth opportunities, but that our model requiring monthly regional meetings was not serving either need. We had been dedicating so much time and energy to sustaining the regional-meeting structure, which was complicated and overwrought, that we had not noticed that our central goals had gotten lost.

As I noted earlier, it is important for leaders to build evaluation into program plans at the point of inception, rather than launching a program with the expectation that an evaluation strategy will be created or will emerge somewhere down the line. Cahalan writes, "A good rule to follow is to build evaluation into project activities, not onto them."[23] Last year I led the creation of a new field education course at my seminary that was markedly different from the previous course. I had worked during the previous year with a team to develop a set of outcome goals, one being that the course should help students connect classroom learning with theological field education experiences. During the first year of the course, I worked with a Web-based instrument called Journey Mapping, through which students could complete Web journals about their experiences in field education in general and in this new course in particular. The guiding questions in the Web journals included requests for examples of the ways that students were starting to see connections between the classroom and the ministry field. I required that students submit journal entries monthly as part of their field education requirement, thus building into the course itself a way to gather information from students.

The results of students' participation in Journey Mapping were mixed, however. Even though I had built data collection into something we were already doing, some submissions were rich and others flimsy. Several students complained that writing the journal entries was tedious and time consuming. Furthermore, still more students wanted to know why they were being asked to submit work they saw as tantamount to course evaluations every month. Through this feedback I was reminded that for many, evaluation is a chore. For others, it carries a veiled threat of dire consequences, even if the person who perceives the threat does not know who or what might be threatened. I explained to students that they should view Journey Mapping as a metaphorical meat thermometer for both the course they were taking and for their own progress in field education. We wanted to have information about how things were cooking while we still had time to adjust the temperature. Still, students did not embrace participation, and generally participants in religious organizations, as I pointed out in chapter 1, can be resistant to built-in evaluation methods. Perhaps not fully understanding how such evaluation can strengthen communities, they see submitting their input as tedious. Or perhaps not believing that their input will be included in decision making, they see participation as a waste of time. Leaders who build evaluation into programs must prepare themselves for resistance and communicate clearly the purpose of ongoing assessment.

That said, however, leaders in religious organizations are busy—very busy. They must take advantage of every possible opportunity to work smarter rather than harder. By building evaluation into new and renewed program designs, leaders accomplish many feats at once:

1. They are able to blend the visioning process crucial to institutional change with the beginnings of an evaluation plan.
2. They articulate what a program is and is not in a way that focuses their energies and their constituents' expectations.
3. They have time to build data collection into what they do every day, so that when a formal evaluation comes along,

they pull data together and analyze the information rather than starting from scratch.

4. They have a constant reminder, in the structure of the program they are creating or sustaining, that the process is not all that matters, even though it takes up much of their time. Rather, the outcome—the prize—is rooted in the deeper meaning that comes from personal and communal transformation.

Case Study: The Program Time Forgot

Leonora is the executive director of Hope Springs, an after-school program for elementary school children in the center of a mid-sized city. The program is housed in the basement of a nonde-nominational Christian church located at a busy intersection. Congregation leaders had founded Hope Springs approximately twenty years earlier as a means for reaching out to the local community. In its early days, Hope Springs offered after-school care to a wide range of families by providing a sliding fee scale and special rates for second and third children in a family. The original motivation for creating Hope Springs came from the church's sense of mission that it needed to help families trying to support themselves while living in the center of an increasingly expensive urban area.

The population of children served, over time, began to come increasingly from lower-income families. As the number of families requiring reduced fees increased, the church could not provide the financial means to continue the program, so a separate board sought and acquired not-for-profit status for Hope Springs as a discrete entity. In that way the program was able to attract both private donations and local governmental support, and it continued to serve the population with the greatest need. But because Hope Springs began to receive public funding, its connection to the church, by necessity, became more distanced.

Leonora, now in her sixth year of leadership, did what she could to maintain a cordial relationship with the church staff. One day, when she went upstairs to retrieve a delivery, she saw a puzzling poster on the church office bulletin board. It appeared to be blueprint plans for a renovation of some kind. She asked the church administrator what she was looking at, and the administrator gleefully described the new education wing that the church planned to add, building on what was now its parking lot. Leonora asked when this renovation would take place and learned that money was already coming in.

Leonora was struck dumb. First, the renovation would be taking place in the space directly adjacent to Hope Springs. Second, families relied on the church parking lot for safe pick-ups and drop-offs. Even worse, during the after-school program hours, part of the parking lot was reserved for basketball, jump rope, and hopscotch, as the urban setting provided no space for a playground. Leonora knew that she needed to talk with church leaders, to remind them that Hope Springs had grown out of the church's mission and could not be forgotten now. As she prayed to God to help her know the right way to approach these leaders, she felt sad and empty: How could we have grown so far apart that we could have just been forgotten this way?

Discussion Questions

- What steps along the way might account for this distanced relationship? When and how might that distancing have been avoided?
- What role do you think Hope Springs plays in the life of the church that founded it? What role could it play?

Chapter 5

∽

Backing In
A Practices Approach

WE HAVE NOW EXPLORED THE ELUSIVE NATURE OF
clarity in postmodern religious organizations, theological perspectives on clarity, evaluation practices, and planning principles.
Now we must ask ourselves this question: Is ministry really all
about programs? Is that all there is to life in a faith community,
one program after another? In one sense, ministry is all about programs. In another sense, it has nothing to do with programs.

In this chapter, I explore this conundrum by describing a theme
that weaves itself throughout both theology as an academic field
and the work of ministry: the thought habit of "backing in." Ministry programs might be intrinsically good on many levels, but
what makes them different from their secular counterparts is the
theological foundation upon which they are built. The ministry programs themselves and their theological grounding must
be considered in tandem if we are to further God's purposes in
the world and to ensure that ministry programs do not lose their
spiritual footing. How do we get to that theological foundation?
By "backing in"—beginning with the outcroppings of a program
and then making our way back to the program's theological foundation—we can understand better how the program furthers a
ministry or mission.

What does "backing in" mean in the context of planning and
evaluating programs? In chapter 3 I discussed logic models. In

describing how to use them, I explained that the first step is to start at the last step, to ask, What would success look like if it happened? What outward and visible signs would tell you that you were meeting your goal? I argued that, ironically, discussion about final outcomes should be the first step in casting a vision for a ministry program. I extend this argument into this chapter by contending that leaders in faith communities can understand the interaction between ministry programs and theological principles by starting with what they see happening in their faith communities and then backing in (or "backing up," or "drilling down"—whatever image helps us understand that we must reconnect with the program's ministry purpose) from there to the theological meaning behind what they see. Faith communities' continual grounding in theological principles is what distinguishes them from secular organizations, and that grounding is the means whereby programs become much more than simple collections of activities.

The Faith Practices Approach

I alluded in the previous section to theological scholarship, suggesting that "backing in" relates to the academic study of religion. I meant by that reference to point toward the rise of the discipline of practical theology. Theological schools such as Candler (at Emory University) and the Boston University School of Theology are turning their attention to practical theology as an essential component of training for ministry in the church and the world. The only difference between practical and classical theology— or perhaps one might say the only difference upon which scholars agree—is a starting point: practical theology begins with the lived experience of human beings seeking a life of faith and then "backs in" to what those lived behaviors and challenges say about the meaning of life. Conversely, the classical study of theology involves doctrines, or ideas; beginning with those, it only later applies them to real-life situations.

I first encountered practical theology accidentally the year after I graduated from Harvard Divinity School. Harvard has a reputation for heady scholarship and a strong emphasis on the study of religion over and above the study of ministry. That said, I had some wonderful mentors and teachers there who helped prepare me for service in ministry. But it was not until I began my first pastoral position that I discovered a clearly practical approach to theology when the senior pastor with whom I served as assistant pastor selected *Practicing Our Faith: A Way of Life for a Searching People*[1] as the text for our church's adult religious-education group. In this book, edited by scholar and theologian Dorothy C. Bass, I read about the earthiest of human behaviors: honoring the body, hospitality, household economics, saying yes and saying no, keeping sabbath, testimony, discernment, shaping communities, forgiveness, healing, dying well, and singing our lives. This book had a profound effect on my life and ministry in that it exposed me to a way of doing theology that felt accessible to me: we begin with what we do every day and then ask questions about what God, faith communities, and our tradition have to do with those practices.

I finished this book with an embryonic sense of what it might mean to take a faith-practices approach to both ministry and theology, to shape my ministry around particular life-giving practices from the Christian tradition, and to explore my own theological worldview by beginning with what I do every day. I have since delved more deeply into the faith-practices approach. I am working on my third faith-practices grant project with help from the Valparaiso Project on the Education and Formation of People in Faith, which encourages and funds scholarship on this form of practical theology. I am applying principles from *Practicing Our Faith* to a particular faith community. In my first faith-practices project, I created a program through which a group of clergy studied the faith practices of college students in a large state university. In the second, I created a faith-practices program that helped theological field education students in a seminary to think theologically about their experiences. Today I am working with a congregation as it develops a faith-practices initiative for younger adults.

I see significant connections between the faith-practices approach and program planning and evaluation, and it is these connections that show me how theology and ministry programs interact. Program planning and evaluation in religious organizations require a particular way of thinking, the one I call "backing in." When I use that expression, I mean that the researcher, leader, or ministry program participant begins by investigating the program itself: What are people doing? How are they behaving? In what are they participating? Only after that initial investigation does one ask questions about what those activities, behaviors, and program components mean on a deeper, theological, meaning-of-life level. I believe that this way of thinking both mirrors the faith-practices approach and can be strengthened by the study of faith practices in the ways I describe next.

First, although faith practices are a set of perspectives on the study of religion, *there is nothing abstract about them*. Dorothy Bass and Craig Dykstra, in their co-written introduction to *Practicing our Faith*, write that avoiding abstraction is one of their primary goals.[2] Rather than lay out inaccessible principles, they succinctly define what makes a practice a practice:

- Practices address fundamental human needs through concrete actions.
- Practices are done in community over time.
- Practices are both ordinary and entangled with God's involvement in our lives.[3]

Therefore, faith practices, much like programs, have specific components and an infrastructure that unifies various practices into a systematic whole. They are made manifest; that is, they are not simply ideas, but ideas-on-the-ground. They also, Dykstra and Bass point out, "possess standards of excellence," through which people can have meaningful conversation about whether the practices are lived out well or badly. This is part and parcel of their very earthiness.

We can use many of these same frames of reference when we think about ministry programs, beyond planning and evaluation. Programs take the form of concrete actions, not just good ideas. They require leaders and participants to work together, not in a one-shot manner but in a sustained relationship. Ministry programs seek to embody God's presence and God's will, even though their very structures might seem secular to an outside observer. And, like faith practices, programs can either further a faith community's vision or fail to do so. Just as the intersection of theology and lived experience is practice, the point where ministry ideas and the drive to meet human needs meet in a faith community is a program. This is the first connection.

The second connection relates to busyness. Bass and Dykstra write, "Lacking a vision for a life-giving way of life, we turn from one task to another, doing as well as we can but increasingly uncertain about what doing things well would look like. All the while, an uneasiness lies just beneath the surface—an uneasiness made of personal restlessness, worry about our loved ones, and apprehension about the well-being of the world."[4] By rooting our human activity in our faith tradition, not acting arbitrarily but being grounded in a deep sense of meaning, we bring order out of our busy activities. Similarly, by grounding ministry programs in an overarching vision, we can encourage our faith communities toward a life of integrity. I use the word integrity here in its traditional sense, which shares a root with "integration." All activities flow into a greater whole: a clear vision for what the faith community seeks to achieve through programs.

A third point of connection between faith practices and program planning and evaluation is perhaps the most obvious. Dykstra and Bass propose three forms of programs that can help individuals build a life around faith practices, both individually and in community. "[O]ur aim is not only to foster good conversations, as nourishing as they are," they write. "Our deepest and dearest purpose is to contribute to the search that is going on all around us. . . . We hope that talk about practices can make a difference in the way people walk with one another and with God."[5] Bass and Dykstra go on to propose educational programs, renewal-oriented justice programs, and faith practices in everyday life as three means through which a person or community can grow in the practice of the Christian faith.

In the years since *Practicing Our Faith* was published, the Valparaiso Project has lived into these suggestions for encouraging growth in faith practices. It has supported a number of program initiatives, including scholarly projects such as full-length books on various faith practices and grants that have enabled faith communities and institutions to bring about social renewal through faith practices. These grant programs help us see that ministry programs and faith practices are not opposites, nor are they like apples and oranges, defying comparison.

Faith practices are like ministry programs in that they are (1) concrete actions, rather than abstract principles, and (2) held together by a broader and loftier vision, rather than being simply a set of disjointed, busy behaviors. Faith practices can also become ministry programs, as we see in the next section.

A Case Study: First Church in Cambridge

As we continue our exploration of the ways that ministry is all about programs, and not at all about programs, I introduce a church that has put together a set of program offerings that are deeply Christian and grounded in theology. First Church in Cambridge (FCC), a United Church of Christ congregation in Massachusetts, provides an example of a church that "backed in" from vision to programs with the help of faith practices. This church illustrates the ways that programs can take on an intentionally theological dimension that elevates them out of the realm of busy activity and into an integrated, faithful way of life.

It is difficult to identify a single starting point for the journey into faith practices and new programs at FCC. When the pastors of that congregation came as guest speakers for my spring 2008 course on program planning and evaluation at Andover Newton,[6] they began their account with the story of a small group conceived by a member of the congregation called the Daughters of Abraham. In this group, the first of many chapters to spring up around the Boston area after September 11, 2001, women from the Christian, Muslim, and Jewish traditions gathered informally and talked about their lives. Senior Pastor Mary Luti said that FCC women who participated came away from that experience with what she called "practice envy." Whereas Jewish and Muslim women in the group were able to define clearly the ways in which their faith intersected with their daily lives, the Christian women in the group found it difficult to describe what made their lives Christian.

In 2002, at about the time participants in the Daughters of Abraham were raising questions about FCC's effectiveness in teaching parishioners about Christianity as a part of ordinary life, FCC leaders began what they described as a "prayerful process of self-study and spiritual discernment."[7] Pastor Luti had come to the congregation two years earlier, and the church was discerning a path for its ministry. That "visioning process" resulted in a four-pronged identity statement that lifted up four images: Open Door, Open Spirit, Open Table, and Open Road. The Open Door represented the church's commitment to be open to all people and to learn from them, "making room for new perspectives, ideas, and gifts, not simply expecting new folks to conform to 'how we do things here.'"[8] Open Spirit represented a commitment to life-long formation in faith. Open Road symbolized building bridges between the church and the wider community. The Open Table circles back to welcoming, pointing to communion as the ritual through which all become one in Christ.

As FCC's leaders began to consider ways in which the church might live out these values, a member learned about the Valparaiso Project's grants program supporting the promotion of faith practices as a means for deepening a community's life. The church applied successfully for funding to help members live out their Open Door, Open Spirit, Open Table, and Open Road vision. FCC used the funding to support a number of initiatives that fell neatly into Dykstra and Bass's suggestions for how faith practices can become programs in education, renewal, and faith in daily life.

FCC expanded its adult-formation program[9] to pay deep and careful attention to faith practices, and these opportunities included both grounding in the Christian tradition and application to daily life. In Advent 2005 the church offered an adult series on hospitality. In Lent 2006 adults studied discernment. In Advent 2006 they participated in a course on testimony. Out of these series, small groups of adults seeking to deepen their faith lives began to proliferate. In just one Sunday, small groups met around topics including parenting as a spiritual journey, an exploration of what money means to us as individuals and in our faith lives, and silent prayer.[10] Furthermore, small groups met in members' homes throughout the Cambridge community and beyond to talk about the faith practices described in *Practicing Our Faith*. FCC also used grant money to extend itself into the wider community, living into its commitment to the Open Road. Leaders built a prominent kiosk that proclaimed FCC's vision to the Cambridge population on the church's busy street, and they used grant funds to strengthen its partnership with the Outdoor Church, a ministry to homeless people on the Cambridge Common, just across the street from the church.

Here is one example of an event at FCC that brought together all three means by which a faith practice can be lived out through a ministry program:

[O]n the first Sunday of May, we celebrated our connection to the Outdoor Church, not only by inviting their minister to preach, but by inviting all the kids and adults to share in the act of making sandwiches during worship, in our chancel, right on the communion table. The symbolism of spiritual and physical feeding in memory of Jesus was exquisite. For that Sunday, the bread used in making the sandwiches became the very bread of heaven used in intinction-style communion. What's more, our children teamed up to serve the bread alongside clergy and deacon offering juice and wine. The service offered our entire congregation an incredibly grounded and plainspoken experience of what it means to feed and be fed, and to be the body of Christ.[11]

On one level, a person could easily say that FCC's faith-practices grant enabled the church to offer some good programs. Yet underlying every good thing that the church did were tradition, history, theology, and vision. In this sense, the programs the church offered and is offering are outcroppings, not entities in themselves. Those outcroppings were planned and evaluated, yes, but they were also rooted in something much bigger than any one initiative. Each initiative was a catalyst for a transformative way of living and thinking.

Furthermore, by teaching this new way of living, the church itself has been transformed. Leaders who worked together to write a grant proposal to the Valparaiso Project reported that their planning process led to a sharpening of their commitments and values.[12] Implementing the grant changed the way the church engaged in governance: "[A] benefit of this Valparaiso partnership is the myriad ways in which Christian practices have been infusing our committee meetings and seeping into deeper layers of our congregational life."[13] When FCC's Pastor Luti resigned in May to take a teaching position at a seminary, leaders in the church immediately formed a "discernment committee" to consider how to prepare for calling a new pastor. Their use of the term "discernment" rather than "search" is just one example of how the programs changed the program designers themselves. For not only did they use spiritual language; they also took time to discern before searching, a discipline they had learned through the adult-formation course on discernment.

Just today, I used FCC in a talk I gave as an example of churches that are reaching deep into the Christian tradition to bring about new life. A member of the audience questioned my choice of example, saying that she knows the church is located in an intellectual center where people appreciate knowledge and tradition in a way people elsewhere do not. I countered that all leaders must read their contexts, but that my argument that ministry programs must be built on a deep root system holds true across communities. People do not come to religious communities seeking programs alone. They seek a more meaningful way of life, and programs are one way that they can find that.

Programs: Freeing Catalyst or Controlling Structure?

As we continue to consider the ways in which programs are and are not all there is to ministry in religious organizations, we must raise a question about control. On the one hand, program infrastructures are things, metaphysical objects; they lack any inherent agenda or power unto themselves. We believe Kathleen Cahalan when she writes in *Projects That Matter*, "Projects are, quite simply, a response to a condition or set of conditions. Projects are strategies and solutions that an organization believes can best address needs, bring awareness to important issues, or answer questions."[14] But we must also remember that projects, or programs, are a means through which leaders create a system whereby they exert power and control. When leaders in a religiously based food program transform an informal vegetable-garden swap into a funded, formal outreach initiative, the swap program can grow and improve. But by adding structure and resources, leaders also create the need for oversight and continued attention.

Nick Carter, president of Andover Newton Theological School, likes to use the aphorism, "To fail to plan is to plan to fail."[15] I agree with him. I also know, however, that leaders who press the importance of planning run three risks:

1. *Their constituents cast them as controlling and uncaring about the role of the Holy Spirit.* Not every member of a faith community thinks like a planner. Some people truly prefer to live in the moment and are confused when their leader wants to look too far ahead. I have learned—often the hard way—that as a leader I must not brush past people who feel this way, for they often have great wisdom to offer about the way the Holy Spirit is available to us only in the present moment.

2. *They can miss out on new opportunities by overstructuring the organization's plan.* People tend to move in and out of ministry programs. When leaders nail down too much of a program's plan, without leaving room for those who might enter the scene with new ideas—or leave the scene, taking their ideas with them—they limit their own effectiveness. It is for this reason that I believe a simple long-term plan designed to be adapted midcourse, coupled with ongoing evaluation, is the best level of structure for a program's plan.

3. *Constituents in religious organizations can be quick to accuse their leaders of being too corporate-minded.* I once served a church whose membership rolls were out of date. The board of deacons formed a small task force to address the issue, and I sat in on its meetings. The church paid denominational membership dues in an amount based on its number of active members, a fact the committee was fairly certain inactive members did not know. The group was able to eliminate about twenty families easily, knowing that members had moved away or died, but after that point it became stuck. No one felt comfortable asking inactive members if they wished to stay on the rolls. One member of the task force suggested writing a letter to inactive members, seeking information

about their plans to continue as participants. Some thought this approach seemed impersonal and cold, not unlike sending an eviction notice, whereas others thought it would be an efficient and face-saving method to enable families no longer involved to move on. The group never got through this impasse, and to this day the membership rolls have not been culled beyond those who have died or moved away.

These three objections raised by constituents about the structure that comes with planning are worthy of the leader's consideration. On one hand, leaders should not be deterred from their efforts to help congregations live out their missions simply because some fear the control that comes with structure. On the other hand, leaders are wise to remember that not everything has to be planned and structured. As a natural-born planner, I find it difficult to say so, but I do believe that we can overstructure programs to their detriment. In my own mind, I have to discipline myself to recognize when I am planning in order to improve a program and when I am planning merely to feed my own illusion of control. The great irony is that the best way for leaders to address these concerns is not to cease planning efforts, but literally to plan "letting go" into program structures.

Control is not the goal of program planning and evaluation. We seek through planning to coordinate our activities around a vision, rather than engaging in a haphazard frenzy of activities. Leaders must invite the Holy Spirit into their program plans—a step that means letting go of control and allowing new life to be infused into programs without the leaders' moderating or mediating every change and new idea. What does this letting go look like? How can leaders provide room in program plans for the Holy Spirit to enter and for the program to take on a life of its own?

In my experience, five attributes of program initiatives can enable us to remain open to the work of the Spirit, rather than creating programs that are overstructured and leader-controlled. These attributes help distinguish ministry programs from programs in a secular setting, as they both make programs transformative and create space for God to work through the program. When leaders take these attributes into consideration, they can serve as lifegiving catalysts for programs in religious organizations.

Programs That Make Use of the Arts

The arts can help programs in religious organizations maintain their connection to the Holy Spirit and remain open to change over time. Music, film, painting, sculpture, dance, and other arts give participants opportunities to engage in nonverbal communication. Because so much of program planning and evaluation makes use of words, the inclusion of arts in the program usually requires some discipline. But when those participating in programs have the opportunity to use the arts in their worship, study, outreach, and daily lives beyond formal programs, they are enriched in ways that are difficult to predict but almost always life-giving.

Deep Communication and Personal Transformation

Programs that give participants the opportunity to explore their own experiences and testify to their own transformations are best able to help people welcome the Holy Spirit's activity. In New England, where I live and serve, this concept is difficult for people to grasp. I have a colleague who grew up in a small Massachusetts town. His father was the Congregational pastor in town, and there was a Southern Baptist congregation down the road. Members of the Congregational parish served by my colleague's father never talked about their faith for fear of being mistaken for Southern Baptists.

My colleague, after entering ordained ministry, decided to pursue doctoral work on the discipline of "theological reflection," because he had always hungered for meaningful conversation about faith and life, and he had never found it in church. Theological reflection is a spiritual discipline in which people consider the events of their lives in light of their faith, asking questions such as "Where was God in that moment?" "What biblical wisdom might provide us with insights about the event?" "What does that event say about life's meaning, about ministry, about who I am and who I am becoming?" They engage in this theological reflection either with a group or one-on-one with a partner, thus strengthening their own faith and growing in relationship with others.

We must recognize that of the people coming to church today, only half or less are attending a congregation in the tradition in which they were raised. This means that increasingly, members of a given congregation are more and more different from one another. People both need and expect deep communication about faith and their life's meaning, if for no other reason than to explore together where God has been in their lives and where God is drawing them. Just last week, in the church I attend, a member offered a "stewardship moment" as part of an October series on giving. She spoke not only about her giving to the church, but also about her faith journey and what had brought her to church in the first place. Her address so moved people that the pastor chose not to offer a sermon, saying, "We have already heard the Word today." And this happened in a stoic, New England congregation where emotional expression in church has historically been viewed with skepticism. Ministry programs that provide opportunities for personal faith exploration and communication have the capacity to bring new life to individuals and to retain the program's connection to the holy.

Engagement with Those Who Are Different

In *Common Fire: Leading Lives of Commitment in a Complex World*,[16] Sharon Daloz Parks and Laurence Parks Daloz offer an account of leaders who have brought about meaningful change in the lives of others. The authors argue that the experience these leaders share is an encounter, at some crucial point in their lives, with people very different from themselves. Programs that include opportunities for participants to engage with those who come from different backgrounds are, by nature, more closely linked with the Holy Spirit. Jesus crossed sociocultural boundaries and engaged—and loved—those in his community whom others would have passed by. When we build into programs opportunities to engage those who are different, we make a bold statement that this program is not about one community, but is concerned with the whole of the human community.

One of the fastest-growing forms of ministry programming today is the "mission trip": members of faith communities travel and serve together with those from different backgrounds. This form of ministry is not without its critics; some call mission trips "tourism in other people's realities," and some criticize those who go on mission trips, judging them to be people seeking a quick fix to make them feel good about themselves. No matter your personal perspective on whether such trips are good, bad, or indifferent, one thing leaders must ask themselves is this: What is it about mission trips that is attracting so many? I would argue that there is something tightly controlled about mission trips—they require vast amounts of planning—but there is also something radically free about them. They remove participants from their comfort zones, quickly cause them to rely on each other, and give them meaningful opportunities to engage those who are different. We can see through the popularity and proliferation of mission trips that these opportunities feed a deep hunger. How can we take that hunger into consideration as we plan all sorts of ministry programs?

Retrieval of the Tradition

FCC's former pastor, Mary Luti, offered the address at Andover Newton's commencement in 2008 on the importance of critically and creatively retrieving the Christian tradition and bringing it to life in ministry today. She used this illustration as she began:

When she was called as FCC's senior pastor, she succeeded a beloved minister who had died of cancer while on medical leave. A parishioner came to see Pastor Luti to describe a worship service that this predecessor had instituted in the church and that the parishioner hoped would continue. Pastor Luti asked for some information about the service, and the parishioner described an event not long after Christmas, when the church was filled with candles and members walked in procession through the dark places of the church, holding lit candles. Pastor Luti said, "This sounds like Epiphany." The parishioner's eyes lit up. "Yes! That's what Pastor called it!" In her address, Pastor Luti went on to urge seminary graduates to go out into the world and "Invent Epiphany!"

By digging deeply into the rich resources of the Christian tradition, leaders who plan ministry programs can build upon centuries of thought, prayer, and process rather than overrelying on their own resources. FCC has a clear commitment to retrieving the Christian tradition in its faith-practices ministry, and the church's fastest-growing population is young adults. I believe this is the case because many young adults feel electronically connected but culturally disconnected from community and tradition. They seek ministry programs infused with respect for heritage and tradition, and ministry programs that attend to this need.

Willingness to Risk Everything

Ministry programs help faith communities make their way toward a vision. They are not ends in themselves, but are rather a means to human transformation and healing in the world. Yet we all know programs that have taken on lives of their own, not in a positive, Holy Spirit–infused way, but rather in a destructive way. Programs that no longer serve the organization's mission and that are sustained out of either comfort with the status quo or fear of change can become like idols. We continue them or allow them to continue, and they drain us of energy. It is my conviction that leaders of ministry programs who state clearly that they are open to allowing a program to die are the leaders most open to the will of the Holy Spirit. At the outset of new programs, leaders are wise to say, "This program will continue as long as it is serving God and the vision of this community, and after that point, it will end."

In fact, I would argue that religious communities that make that very statement about themselves—we will exist as a faith community as long as doing so serves God and the community's vision, after which point our church will die—are the most authentically Christian communities. For if we truly believe in the power of the resurrection, we are all already dead and risen in Christ. So our ministry programs, and even our faith communities, are risen in Christ and impervious to threat. We create programs, we run them, and when they have served their purpose, we bring them to an end. But they never truly die in God's eyes.

Is Ministry All about Programs?

Ministry programs are the means by which the care, compassion, vision, and purpose of a faith community are delivered. If we want to know what a religious organization stands for, we should start with the programs it offers and then "back in" to understand what the organization believes. Programs are the visible outcropping of how a faith community understands God's purpose for it. All this said, programs are not ends in themselves; rather they are a means, and when we confuse the ends with the means, we ultimately fail to live into the calling of leadership in a faith community. For leadership in a faith community requires constant openness to God's will, and structured programs sometimes fail to remain open in crucial ways.

Sometimes constituents in religious organizations express discomfort with planning because they fear it will lead to closed, overstructured programs. This concern is legitimate, but rather than avoid planning to ensure that we remain open to change, we can build into programs disciplines that help us remain open to the Holy Spirit's work. By including the arts, structuring opportunities for deep sharing, providing engagement with those who are different from us, critically and creatively retrieving wisdom from the faith tradition, and clearly stating that programs are meant to continue only so long as they serve a missional purpose, we build openness into programs. Leading with this sort of intentionality helps us avoid both the trap of failing to plan so as to seem open and the trap of creating programs that are structured to the point that they fail to invite the Spirit in.

So I close with the words that began this chapter: In one sense, ministry is all about programs. In another, it has nothing to do with programs. Without programs, faith communities lack a "docking system" between their vision for the world God intends for us and the very world they seek to heal and change. But programs themselves are not the end-all and be-all. Rather, they are the living manifestation of the one End-All, Be-All: God, and God's son, and God's Spirit. By creating ministry programs designed to be living, three-dimensional, and Spirit-driven, we avoid the trap of thinking that planned programs are by nature only human. Rather, it is possible to build a program that takes into consideration the essential role of the Holy Spirit.

Case Study: Dick's Roses

Stephen was pastor of First Presbyterian Church in Avondale, known around town as "First Pres," for six years before he asked the question: Why do we place a rose on the chancel when a new baby is born to a family in the congregation?

Before coming to First Pres, Stephen had served as an associate pastor for a growing and lively congregation, Faith Presbyterian, also in Avondale. His senior pastor colleague there, Amy, had a love for worship and Christian history, and she brought to her work a deep appreciation for the faith tradition and the roots of the practices in which they engaged. Whenever she preached at Faith—about three times a month—she taught the congregation why traditions were in place, not just in that congregation but in

Christian practice. Stephen learned a great deal from her and was astonished by how little he had known about his own faith tradition before arriving at Faith.

Because Faith was so close to First Pres, Stephen was well aware that First Pres had the reputation of being a stoic worshiping congregation with a great love for Presbyterian "decency and order." When the solo pastor position became available there, Stephen felt compelled to apply, even with this knowledge. First Pres was the only other church in town where Stephen could envision serving, and relocating was not an option; his wife was from Avondale, and as they began to talk about starting a family, leaving her hometown was not something she wanted. Stephen worried about what it would be like to go to a more formal congregation. Faith had been like a second seminary experience for him, and he knew he would miss it. It had become in his mind the example of what an emotionally open and tradition-loving church could be.

Now, six years later, he was becoming used to First Pres's ways. He liked that the church leadership was strong and that boards functioned with little prodding from him. Although he was occasionally frustrated by the general apathy in the church toward adult Christian education, he appreciated that the members loved their children and ran the best Sunday school in town. After years of frustration with infertility, Stephen and his wife were expecting their first child through adoption in a few months.

It was only then, when Stephen started thinking about welcoming his own child into the congregation, that he thought to ask: Why do we place a rose on the chancel when a new baby comes? He posed this question to Marjorie, the eighty-two-year-old leader of the flower committee who had served in this capacity for more than forty years. Stephen expected Marjorie to say that a member of the congregation had seen this tradition in another church, liked it, and brought it back. He knew of many churches that placed roses on the chancel on occasions like these. But Marjorie surprised him:

Well, Pastor, you never got a chance to meet Dick Whidmore. Dick was a member here up until 1971 or so, when he died, and he was an elder and the superintendent of the Sunday school. He and his wife, Irma, never had kids, but they lived just down the street from the church. Kids from Sunday school were in and out of Dick and Irma's house all the time. The first youth group meetings the church ever had started there. They had a beautiful fenced-in yard with rose bushes lining it all around. Every time Dick heard that a new baby had come, he'd cut a rose and bring it with him to church. You see, he almost always found out about the babies before the pastors did, because Irma was a nurse down at General Hospital, so he got the inside information. In the wintertime, Irma insisted that he bring a silk rose, so the January babies didn't get left out.

After Dick died, someone else started providing roses; we don't actually know who. They would just be up there, before we even set up the flowers. Then that stopped, and Joe Friend, who was in Dick Whidmore's very first youth group, started bringing them. Now that Joe's family has moved away, I take care of it, because Dick was the one who invited me to teach Sunday school for the first time. When I die, I hope someone else is here to take it over, because it really is one of our church's traditions that makes me feel that this is my home.

Discussion Questions

- Are there traditions in your congregation of which the story of Dick's roses reminds you?
- If you were Stephen, how might you incorporate this tradition into your ministry? In what way could you "use" this story? Would you fear "abusing" this story?
- What are the parallels between the rose on the chancel and other church traditions at First Pres? At Faith? How are traditions like these different from, and similar to, faith practices like prayer or communion?

Chapter 6

~

Turning the Lens on Ourselves
Our Lives as Programs We Lead

LAST DECEMBER, HAVING ALREADY WRITTEN ABOUT a fictional church fair in chapter 1, I experienced a church-fair conundrum all my own. I enjoy my involvement in our local United Church of Christ congregation, but as an ordained person in the pews I have to take care where and how I get involved. I never want to undermine our beloved pastor, first of all, and my family benefits from my taking a layperson's role in the congregation. That said, most of the typical activities of mothers in our church do not play to my strengths. I am not "crafty" at all, enjoy but do not adore small children (except for my own, of course), and do not gravitate to social functions as much as to worship activities. I try my best to stay involved in activities at the church so as to support the ministry, even if certain activities more typical of women my age are not a great fit for me.

The leader of our church fair is another mother in the congregation whom I like and respect. As she coordinated activities leading up to the fair, she did not specifically ask me for help, probably knowing more than the average church member about what I do and do not enjoy by way of church activities. One source of frustration for me, as someone outside the planning loop, was that, in any church announcement about the fair, no one ever announced its date. We are new enough to the church that we do not know the regular rhythm of the year. Newsletter, bulletin, and spoken announcements varied in style, but they were consistent in that one attribute: not one of them told us when the fair would take place.

Of course, I could have made more of an effort to find out the date with a simple e-mail or phone call, but I was overwhelmed with other things. Our daughter has started to take a keen interest in karate, and she was getting ready to change to a new, more advanced class. I had offered to help coordinate an alumni event for my undergraduate college for families in the Boston area. Our twin godchildren were about to celebrate a birthday, just two weeks after that of our own daughter. And of course my semester at Andover Newton was wrapping up, bringing all of the busyness natural to the end of a term.

By now, you may have already guessed what I am about to reveal: When I learned the date of the church fair, I realized that it:

- Was taking place on the same day as the alumni event I was helping to plan.
- Was also conflicting with our godchildren's birthday party.
- Overlapped directly with the first meeting of our daughter's new karate class.

Of course, this schedule conflict by no means qualifies as an emergency situation. Rather, it was a typical situation for today's families: many competing time commitments, all related to different values and priorities. We are lucky people, to be sure, to have so many activities we enjoy. But how do we make good decisions on a daily basis when life is so complicated and when those about whom we care and who care about us place different demands upon us? My church-fair conundrum relates in part to the complexity in the lives of congregations everywhere, but it also connects to the complexity in my own mind that I must manage daily. How can the principles of evaluation and program planning help us not just as leaders in faith communities, but as individual people of faith trying to make our way in this life?

Clarity in Leaders' Lives

Last week, a denominational leader called to let me know that she had referred one of the ministers in her care to me for some conversation and advice. The minister had been called to a newly created role in a denominational office, and she had been charged not only with creating a new program but also with figuring out that program's vision. The position would require creativity and energy, but it would also call upon the leader to move quickly from big ideas to a workable infrastructure. In my experience, it is rare to find one person who is in equal measure creative and pragmatic, but these qualities would be necessary for the newly called minister to thrive. When I asked the denominational leader, "Why send her to me, an academic who writes about administrative leadership for ministry, rather than to a ministry colleague or spiritual director?" she said, "This new minister just has so much going on in her head." I took this to mean that the minister had many great ideas, but no plan to put legs underneath those ideas. She needed help prioritizing, strategizing and—most relevant to this chapter—clarifying her thoughts.

Throughout this book, I have argued that congregations and other faith communities have, as the denominational leader might have put it, "a lot going on in their heads," more ideas or activities than a leader can "eyeball" or assess purely with the help of "gut reactions." I have proposed that principles from program planning and evaluation can help a leader make sense of his or her community in a way that brings about new clarity, and therefore more integrity and effectiveness. I make a related argument later in this chapter: program planning and evaluation can also help the leader make sense of himself or herself. It is by no means original for me to argue that the internal clarity of the leader has an effect on faith communities, however, as other authors and faith communities discovered long ago that the leader's groundedness has everything to do with his or her effectiveness as a leader and the health of the whole institution.

Edwin Friedman's "Self-differentiated Leader"

Edwin H. Friedman, a rabbi, counselor, and scholar of family systems, wrote extensively about the importance of the leader's internal clarity to the life of the institution she or he leads. In his final work, *A Failure of Nerve: Leadership in the Age of the Quick Fix*,[1] Friedman argues that a leader's "self-differentiation" is the key to his or her ability to serve, challenge, and lead an institution toward meaningful change. He defines self-differentiation this way:

1. The leader is clear about his or her life goals.
2. The leader can separate herself or himself from the community, capable both of thinking independently and of remaining connected in a community.
3. The leader can maintain a nonanxious yet challenging presence within the community.
4. The leader can manage his or her own reactivity—or strong emotional responses—as well as the reactivity of others, making it possible for the leader to displease others without losing himself or herself.[2]

Friedman places little stock in data-driven decision making for leaders, arguing that more information is not as important for leaders as decisiveness and emotional maturity are.[3] He defines emotional maturity as "the willingness to take responsibility for one's own emotional being and destiny."[4] Leaders need a clearer sense of who they are, where they end and their communities begin, and an ability to remain nonanxious even in the face of sabotage.

In a "stuck system,"[5] when an institution is unable to make meaningful changes—even changes that would save the institution from extinction—trying harder or gathering more information is not the answer. "[M]ore learning will not, on its own, automatically change the way people see things or think. There must first be a shift in the emotional processes of that institution."[6] That shift begins with the leader's finding his or her own self, even in the midst of connection and relationship. When the leader finds a voice, claims individuality, and demarcates where she or he begins and where others end, this self-differentiation brings catharsis to the whole community. Ultimately, Friedman argues, finding clarity within oneself is not part of the work of the leader; rather, it is leadership.

Internal Clarity and Boundaries

This argument—that the leader's self-differentiation is a key to his or her effectiveness—resonates with Scott Cormode's work, described in earlier chapters, about spiritual sense-making as a function of ministerial leadership. Friedman's argument about self-differentiated leadership also connects with concepts one learns about in the study of professional boundaries. Especially in light of clergy sexual abuse scandals, but also in light of many pastors' difficulties understanding the appropriate distance to keep from their congregations, more and more denominations are requiring that pastors become trained in maintaining professional boundaries. To maintain healthy boundaries, or to understand where the leader ends and the community begins, requires reflection and internal clarity.

In the FaithTrust Institute's training manual for those who teach clergy about boundaries, one reads that ordained ministers often find themselves in "dual relationships," where "a person attempts to fulfill two roles with the same person—for example, to have a professional and a personal relationship with the same person."[7] The manual offers examples of dual relationships for clergy, such as "a minister who becomes a close family friend of a family in his congregation" and "a minister who serves as pastor to his/her own family."[8] The manual does not state that having a dual relationship is in itself a boundary violation, but rather that dual relationships are fertile soil in which a violation could

reasonably flourish: "When a minister attempts a dual relationship with a congregant, client, employee, student, or staff member, the ministerial relationship is in jeopardy."[9]

When I offer training on boundaries to field education students
at Andover Newton, the first thing I tell them is that they should
not understand professional boundaries as something meant to
protect *them*. Professional clergy must have good boundaries in
order to protect *their congregations*. From whom, you might ask?
From the clergy themselves: ministers whose lack of differentiation would lead parishioners into boundaryless, and therefore
possibly abusive, relationships. Often ordained ministers use the
term "boundaries" to describe taking care of themselves. Self-
care is not irrelevant to boundary management by any means. As
Friedman argues, leaders must be able to distinguish their own
goals and wishes from those of others, and to separate from others while remaining connected. No one can accomplish those
two purposes without downtime and good physical and mental
health. That said, the crucial attribute of professional boundaries
that ministerial leaders must understand is that their first obligation is to serve, not to be served by, those to whom they minister.

The chair of a church's stewardship committee might find herself asking a next-door neighbor to increase his pledge. A pastor
in a small town might have no choice but to take his children to
a pediatrician who is also a church member. One of the ways in
which ministerial leadership differs from other professional relationships is that dual relationships are not only common: they are
inevitable. What therapist ever finds herself counseling a battered
wife one morning and then serving on a committee with the bat-
tering husband the same evening? Such a bind is typical for a pastor. What attorney is asked by a client to attend a family birthday
party? Again, ministerial leaders are constantly—even blessedly—
treated as family friends. To name the difficulties of dual relationships, and to find internal clarity about where the edges meet and
overlap within those relationships, helps the leader not just to be

more effective, but to provide leadership through the nonanxious presence Friedman describes.

Methods of Discernment

Throughout this book I have argued that religious organizations today, and the communities that surround them, are too complicated for a leader to analyze without the help of some intentional practices, some of which I lift up in earlier chapters: logic models, stakeholder maps, data-collection strategies, and condition/intervention diagrams. Many religious communities have, over time, come to see that people of faith as individuals also need intentional practices that help them find clarity in their lives. Some faith traditions have created methods of discernment for that purpose. Discernment is the practice that helps a person like me determine whether to volunteer at the church fair, take her daughter to karate, support an alumni event, or attend her godchildren's birthday party—when all are happening on the same day. Discernment also requires discipline to help the faithful person stay grounded in God and avoid self-deception.[10]

In his chapter on discernment in the anthology *Practicing Our Faith: A Way of Life for a Searching People*, Frank Rogers, a Roman Catholic layperson who teaches religious education, writes that discernment helps us with inner confusion, when we do not know what we want to do, and with confusion thrust upon us from outside ourselves, when we become confused by the mixed signals that we receive and seek to interpret.[11] When we discern, Rogers writes, we as individuals or as participants in whole communities seek to participate in God's will for our lives.[12] Rogers describes two methods of discernment from different corners of the Christian tradition that offer insights into how Christians have, over time, used intentional practices to find greater clarity in their lives.

Jesuit Practices of Discernment

Anyone who has worked with a Jesuit spiritual director can tell
you: When it comes to discernment, nobody does it better. Ignatius of Loyola, sixteenth-century founder of the Jesuit movement
within the Roman Catholic Church, taught his followers a step-
by-step method for making decisions that is practiced to this day.
Many of the good habits for discernment that we hear about in
daily living, such as lists of pros and cons, find roots in Jesuit spirituality as first described by Ignatius.

Jesuit discernment begins with three dispositions, or prior states
of mind a person must achieve before beginning to discern:

1. A commitment to follow God.
2. An attitude of indifference to every other desire.
3. A sensitivity to God's ways and being, as cultivated by prayer,
   Scripture, and faithful acts.[13]

After these predispositions are taken into consideration, a
person can begin the Jesuit discernment process. In the first step,
the discerner maximizes information that would help him or her
make a better decision. That information can include reading and
research, feedback from wise counselors, and conversation with
others who have faced similar questions. After that first step, the
discerning person considers the negative side by settling into the
direction she or he feels least inclined to pursue. In essence, the
discerner "decides" to pursue the path that seems least appealing
and then examines the feelings that come from that "decision."
After giving due time to the negative side, the discerner then set-
tles into another "decision," this time opting for the course that
seems most appealing. The discerning person again monitors the
feelings that come with mentally pursuing that avenue. Finally,
the discerner makes a tentative decision—this time not for the
sake of argument, but with true intention to follow that course of
action—and sits with that possibility for further reflection.[14]

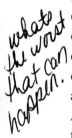
what's the worst that can happen.

Through this Jesuit process of discernment, the person making a decision not only has thought about all relevant options, but has experienced the feelings associated with different courses of action and allowed them to inform his or her choices. Jesuits believe that our feelings are ways in which God communicates with us. By taking our feelings seriously, we invite God's will into our day-to-day decisions, listening to our feelings and seeking within them the direction God would lead us.

Quaker Models of Discernment

It might surprise a reader that it has taken all this time, with a book title like *Holy Clarity*, for me to describe Quaker models of discernment. It is the Quakers, after all, who conceived of "clearness committees" as a way for an individual to come to a decision with the help of a faith community. The Quaker tradition is perhaps the best example of the link between a life of faith and a life of clarity, both in communal and individual lives.

Part of participation in Quaker faith communities includes helping others in the community make decisions through "clearness committees." In this faith practice, a member of a Quaker meeting who must make a decision brings together a group of fellow seekers for a three-hour session. During that time, caring others ask probing questions of the discerner with the hope of drawing out the person's true desires, as well as considering where the Holy Spirit is at work in the life of the discerner. In his book *Let Your Life Speak: Listening for the Voice of Vocation*, scholar of theology and education Parker Palmer describes a clearness committee he brought together essentially to confirm something he had already decided to do: to say yes to an invitation to become a high-profile leader in a prestigious organization. Even in responding to the first few questions of his clearness committee, he was able to uncover the way in which his ego had shouted over the voice of the Spirit, which was telling him that the opportunity was not right for him.[15] As Rogers observes, faith practices help us get past false voices to our true callings.[16]

Quakers embrace careful discernment in their communal lives as well through meetings. In addition to meetings for worship, where Quakers listen to the voice of the Holy Spirit and speak when moved to do so, Quaker communities make decisions through meetings for business. They believe that each person in a meeting has insight into the will of the Holy Spirit from some perspective[17] and, therefore, that making decisions through a group process provides the most accurate interpretation of the Spirit's will for the community. Quakers do not vote on decisions but rather covenant to come to consensus, meaning that even those who hold a view different from that of the rest of the group choose to compromise for the best interests of the community.

Jesuit and Quaker discernment practices share important elements. Both operate on the assumption that God cares about the day-to-day decisions of human beings. Both faith communities seek to consider seriously the will of God, through the Holy Spirit, as they think and reason in intentional ways. Both groups' discernment practices are built on the presupposition that human interpretation of revelation is, by nature, imperfect, and that a person making a decision without the benefit of intentional practices is likely to confuse his or her will, or the will of nefarious others, with the will of the Spirit.

Emotional Systems

One shortcoming of both Jesuit and Quaker practices of discernment is that they operate on the assumption that an individual can discern a correct path for life on his or her own. Jesuits locate discernment within the human mind, and in the context of a prayerful life. Quakers attempt to draw out of one another, with the help of probing questions, what individuals wish to do with their lives. Neither of these models pays adequate attention, however, to the ways in which individuals are intertwined, to the point that self-differentiation must be a prior step to any form of discernment.

Both Jesuit and Quaker practices of discernment could be used by one person or by a group of people in a faith community. Ultimately, although this chapter focuses on clarity within individual leaders, separating individual clarity from clarity in an institution constitutes a false dichotomy. Friedman in particular would argue that clarity in one person in an organization—particularly clarity made manifest in a non-anxious, separate-but-connected leader—has a catalytic effect on the whole community: "Clearly defined, non-anxious leadership promotes healthy differentiation throughout a system, while reactive, peace-at-all-costs, anxious leadership does the opposite."[18] That well-differentiated person need not be the person in the leadership office, however, but can be any person who is able to maintain a differentiated state. To make an argument that individual and institutional clarity are interconnected, one need only consider the way in which a clear-headed leader brings clarity to his or her organization. Friedman would attribute this symbiosis between leaders and individuals to emotional systems.

Emotional systems are groups of people who have developed interdependencies to the point that their relationships have taken on an identity of their own, beyond the individuals participating.[19] Friedman writes that "systems theory," or the study of emotional systems among other forms of human systems, "recognizes society as the product, not the sum, of human relationships."[20] Systems theory relies on a paradigm for making sense of human interactions that differs in three specific ways from the paradigms used in other social sciences. First, systems theory takes for granted that relationships are not the sum of personalities in relationships, but rather exist in a network more complex than the sum of individuals in the system. Second, systems theory treats the past not as prologue, but as present; the past plays an everyday role in emotional systems. Third, systems theory assumes that all life processes—from the smallest cell in the human body to the largest institution, such as a nation—are interconnected.[21]

Friedman writes, "The essential characteristic of systems thinking is that the functioning of any part of the network is due to its position in the network rather than to its own nature."[22] This key concept in systems thinking relates to the interconnection between clarity in the individual and clarity in a system. It is quite possible that an individual who has been utterly clear in previous leadership roles can become confused and unclear in an institution that has struggled with missionlessness over generations. When leaders find themselves unable to find clarity in their work in a particular institution, this difficulty might have more to do with the system than with any individual failings. Systems and individuals are interconnected not through mirroring one another, but rather through being *in* one another, inseparably intertwined.

A leader's self-differentiation and clearheadedness are crucial to an organization's health. Not only do leaders need to state clearly what they see happening in their institutions—making spiritual sense of their circumstances, as Cormode would say—but they must also be aware of emotional systems at work. Therefore, the relationship between emotional systems and holy clarity takes place on two levels. First, a leader's clarity has a clarifying effect on the organization. Second, a leader's awareness of the nature of emotional systems helps the leader to sustain clarity in his or her own life. Many leaders find themselves at the helm of organizations whose internal relationships have taken on lives of their own. Knowing this state of affairs helps the leader to understand the limitations and opportunities present in the midst of emotional systems.

The Limitations of Discernment

The most obvious pitfall of intentional discernment practices in faith communities is that, upon first glance, they look simple. Discernment, however, is never simple and can even be risky and downright painful. The first time I read Friedman's *A Failure of Nerve*, the word "failure" in the title threw me off. I *do* feel like a failure when I am unable to remain as "self-differentiated" as Friedman suggests leaders should be. But as I explored the book more deeply, I found comfort in Friedman's description of the well-differentiated leader: "It is not as though some leaders can do this and others cannot. No one does this easily, and most leaders, I have learned, can improve their capacity."[23]

The second limitation of discernment practices is that their underlying assumptions tend to contradict one another. Even among the few concepts I have introduced in this chapter, disagreements abound when we place the different discernment styles into conversation with another. Consider, for example, Quaker meetings and Friedman's self-differentiated leader. Friedman would likely argue that the Quaker practice of making business decisions by consensus represents an "unreasonable faith in reasonableness."[24] Friedman, throughout *A Failure of Nerve*, argues that well-differentiated leaders are nearly always met with sabotage from those who are less well-differentiated. He also writes that an instinct toward "herding"[25] and away from individuality is one cause of societal regression. For these reasons alone he would likely see consensus-based decision making as an adaptation to the weakest in the group. He calls such adaptation counter-evolutionary and therefore dangerous to societal progress.

A third limitation of any discernment exercise is that, insofar as discernment is just that—an exercise—the practice relies upon imagination and simulation. Those who discern a particular path to follow do not know exactly what following that path will mean, so no matter how careful their research, they deal with limited information. In Jesuit methods of discernment, for example, the participant pretends to make a decision for or against what he or she perceives as the most desirable path and then seeks to garner meaningful information from the emotions arising out of that pretending. Who knows, however, whether the human emotions generated in the context of a simulated experience are genuine, even so genuine as to be called God's will? For example, if someone were to use Jesuit discernment practices to decide whether to end a friendship, that simulation would not take into consideration the friend, whose feelings and reactions would obviously affect the emotional response that is supposed to be so telling.

Discernment practices are not computer programs into which people input data and from which they receive answers. They rely on a certain level of rationality and reasonableness that is not always present in communities or in our very selves. They are not parlor games that are fun and interesting; rather they are difficult and can challenge our most deeply held beliefs. Just as the evaluation and planning exercises described in this book are simple models with complicated implications, discernment practices are easy to learn but as utterly flawed as the fallen human beings who practice them.

Program Planning and Evaluation for Individuals

Rogers's definition of discernment as the practice "by which a community or an individual seeks, recognizes, and intentionally takes part in the activity of God in concrete situations"[26] makes room for the possibility that the program planning and evaluation practices described in this book can be used as methods for discernment. The methods are intentional in that they serve as tools for the person who wishes to find greater clarity. They can be used individually as thought-organizing tools for leaders or collectively in a community of leaders or a group of leaders and constituents. The theological worldview this book has promoted is that we find

God's will when we find clarity: the kingdom of God is, among other attributes, clear. That clarity is beautiful and worthy, but we cannot always find it without effort and careful discernment.

As in previous chapters, I will provide a fictional case study. In addition, however, I will describe how the main characters in the story could make use of program planning and evaluation to find clarity.

Family Commitments

Melody is a 35-year-old mother of two living in a suburban area. She had taught fifth grade in the public schools, but while she was pregnant with her second child, she and her husband, Mitch, had a unsettling surprise. Mitch, an engineer who had always made much more money than Melody, received a negative performance review at his company. In the review, his supervisor criticized how much work he had missed since his son had been born. Mitch believed that his supervisor's reaction was due partly to the company's meager parental-leave benefits for fathers, but it also related to Melody's difficult recovery from a caesarean section. After that review, Mitch and Melody decided together, during a long kitchen-table conversation, that Melody would not go back to work after her second maternity leave, to free up time for Mitch to be at work. Melody would wait until nearly the end of her maternity leave before resigning, however, allowing time for her new medical benefits to kick in and also ensuring that she would not lose her maternity-leave salary, upon which she and Mitch depended.

Melody had mixed feelings about this decision from the start. First, she considered the teachers at her school to be her friends, and by waiting until late in her leave to tell them she was resigning, she basically had to lie to them about her plans. Second, although she was excited to get a respite from teaching, she wondered whether she would ever break back into the job market for teaching. Although there were teacher shortages in some parts of the country, the town where she and Mitch and their son lived was one where people waited for years to tap into the excellent benefits of teaching public school. Finally, leaving her job reintroduced a question that had troubled her throughout her college years: "Am I really called to be a teacher?" Something about teaching had always felt not quite right, but she came from a family of educators—her mother had been superintendent of the school system Melody attended when she was growing up, and her father had been her English teacher—and she had no other clear plans; teaching had always seemed the only way.

After their second child was born, Melody and Mitch began to attend a church in the center of town that had a strong Sunday-school program. Melody had grown up going to a church in the tradition of this congregation, but she had strayed from regular attendance after an ill-fated experiment with a campus ministry group in college. The group, which at first welcomed her with open arms and made her feel at home, had pushed her out when she shared some doubts about the theology the group was promoting. After a dozen years away from organized religion, Melody began to attend a midweek stay-at-home mothers' playgroup at this new church and quickly came to rely on the other mothers in the group as a source of adult stimulation and emotional support. The convener of the group, Amanda, had made career and mothering decisions similar to Melody's and was able to celebrate Melody's joy at being home with her children, as well as to listen nonjudgmentally to Melody's stories of ambivalent feelings about work-related decisions.

It was Amanda who recommended Melody when a position—director of religious education—came open at the church. Melody received a phone call from Pastor Ellen on a particularly difficult day; Mitch had left for work at 6:00 A.M. before their baby and toddler woke up. When they did awake, Melody discovered they both had contracted colds and were sniffly and miserable. She could not take them to playgroup at the church. Staying home meant a loss of companionship for her, but she knew that all she could do was wait—with the expectation that a croupy night was right around the corner. Pastor Ellen could tell right away that it was a tough day to call, but she made it clear that she would like Melody to consider the position at the church. She agreed to send an e-mail with more information.

When Melody read the position description, she felt a stirring in her stomach that had been absent for a long time. The position involved coordinating a staff of volunteer teachers, choosing curricula for the various Sunday school classes and youth fellowship, and leading confirmation class with Pastor Ellen. The part-time position offered a small salary and no health insurance, but it took place mostly on Sundays, when Mitch was home. The only fringe benefit was the opportunity to take one course each semester at the seminary in a nearby town, so that the director could become grounded in the Bible, theology, and religious education theory. Melody responded to the e-mail, before even talking with Mitch, that she would like to be considered for the position.

Melody learned of the opportunity about eight months after the birth of their daughter, and later the same week, Mitch's performance review came around again. He had missed practically no work when the second baby was born, even though Melody had had a second caesarean. Melody's mother, now retired, had stayed with the family for two weeks after the surgery to help Melody at home and to take care of both children. Yet in the review, Mitch's supervisor gave him the same low ratings. This time, the reasoning behind his boss's critique was that Mitch did not work late often enough, or demand enough of those who worked under him. With a second negative performance review, Mitch would receive no merit pay or cost-of-living increase and would put be on formal warning. That gave him six months to improve or to find another position.

Melody and Mitch had to sit down at the kitchen table all over again. They were not sure even where to begin to piece together what they wanted, what they needed, and where they were being called in both work and family life.

Using Program Planning and Evaluation in Our Lives

CONDITION/INTERVENTION

Up to this point, the techniques this book has described have been assumed to be tools a leader uses when making sense of his or her religious organization. But we can use them as tools for discernment in our personal and family lives as well. As I noted earlier, Friedman argues that leaders do not need more information as much as they need decisive means of analyzing information and making the best use of it to move ahead.[27] As leaders of our own lives, we can take advantage of tools that help us organize our thoughts about what we ought to do, or at least help us make sense of what is happening around us.

In the Condition/Intervention exercise, leaders talk first about the state of affairs that concerns them, and then they talk about what they want to do to affect or influence that state of affairs. As they consider these questions, they ask themselves what success would mean if they attained it: What would change in their condition? What would be an intervention they could live with?

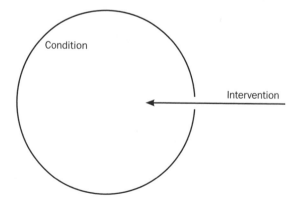

Mitch and Melody can use this exercise in their kitchen-table conversation. By starting with the situation they are in, they can connect with each other and test their perceptions about reality in their household. If they do this, they may uncover two flaws in the logic that led them to this place. First, they invested unreasonable faith in the reasonableness[28] of Mitch's supervisor. They thought that, if Melody left her job and Mitch spent more time at work, his review would improve. This assumption may not have been grounded in reality; it is possible that Mitch's supervisor was impossible to please, or that he adapted his expectations upward after Mitch's last review. A second flaw in their logic was that Melody was leaving her job because she needed to be at home. Logistically, this is true for many families; child care can often be more expensive than families can manage. But in this case, Melody's own vocational questioning also played a role that should be taken into consideration.

When describing the condition, factors like these ought to be part of the picture. When they are, it becomes clear that Mitch and Melody chose an intervention that was not seamlessly connected to the condition they were trying to alleviate. That said, Melody and Mitch would benefit from talking together about how they want to live their lives. Do they feel good about their home life now? Mitch's job satisfaction? Melody's fulfillment? What do their children need from them and from others? And what kinds of changes, or interventions, would help to get them to that aspired-for condition?

In making decisions about Melody's leaving her job, it seems that Mitch and Melody both made the mistake of focusing more on process—what are we going to do?—than on outcome: What do we want our family life to be like? They now have an opportunity to back up and ask—considering that Mitch's boss might never be satisfied and considering that Melody has (finally) discovered something that has piqued her interest: What is it they actually want?—not just what do they want to do, but what life do they want to live?

Logic Models

Once Mitch and Melody have come to some clarity about what kind of home life they would like, and how each of them might find some vocational satisfaction amid their other obligations, they can make use of a logic model as they talk about how they could live into some of their hopes.

RESOURCES	INPUTS	OUTPUTS	IMPACT	INDICATORS

In the "indicators" column, they would list some of the things they would like to see happening in their lives. They then would work backward, considering what those things they see might mean, or their "impact." For instance, if they wish to find greater humor and joy in their parenting lives, what would need to change at home and at work for this aim to be realized? Indicators are outward, visible signs of deep change. Once Melody and Mitch know what they want their lives to look like, they can then ask what underlying change is the precursor to those outward signs. They would consider what needs to go into that impact, "outputs"; namely, what do they have to do to bring about these changes? It is at this point, working backward, that they would test their hopes against reality. Could they afford the "inputs" necessary? Do they have the "resources"? Considering that many of their decisions have clear financial implications, both long- and short-term, this is a crucial step.

Logic models are most helpful when the person using them thinks small and creates several, each for different program components within an organization. For instance, a school might have one logic model for each department. In a family's life, breaking down logic models will look a bit different. In the case at hand, that would mean creating a logic model for Melody, another for Mitch, and one for the household. Here is an example of what Melody's might look like:

RESOURCES	INPUTS	OUTPUTS	IMPACT	INDICATORS
I am offered the position Mitch can take care of the kids Sundays, and I can find child care for the other days and for seminary class time My education degree My interest in this position	I say yes to the job at church I continue to stay home the rest of the time	I work at the church as the religious education director I am a stay-at-home mother four days per week	I am in a stimulating and challenging part-time job that makes use of my background and provides further educational opportunities I am home most days taking care of my kids	I feel that I have found a good fit for my gifts and interests I have a close bond with my children and other mothers

Obviously, Mitch's logic model might look less optimistic. He might simply have a supervisor whom he cannot please or whose standards he cannot predict. The logic model would help Mitch see this, however, and perhaps motivate him to have a concrete conversation with his supervisor about the specific parameters that will guide the next review in six months. It might also uncover the awareness that Mitch no longer wants to work in this setting, a decision that would have implications for all in the family.

STAKEHOLDER MAPS

The Quaker discernment practice of clearness committees brings together groups of people who help individuals make decisions through asking open-ended questions. Jesuit discernment first calls upon the discerner to gather as much information as possible before making a decision. Stakeholder mapping provides discerning people with a tool for organizing resources for discernment. It also can help someone seeking to make a decision to consider the other people whom the decision will affect.

Mitch and Melody could use a stakeholder map in both ways. On one map, they would place in the center circle the names of those who would be most affected by their choices, and in the outer circles the names of those who would be affected, but less so. On the second map, they would place in the inner circle the names of the most helpful sources of support and advice, working their way outward to those with less directly helpful insights to share.

Mitch and Melody's decisions will affect many people, and in fact they have already had an effect. First, their children will feel the impact of their parents' choices, whether or not they are aware of it. The school Melody left had to fill a vacancy on short notice and to pay out benefits to a teacher who did not return to work. Mitch's company had to work around his absences for at

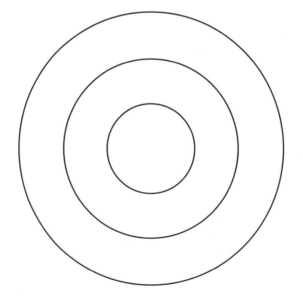

least a short time. Pastor Ellen "needs" something from Melody, and Melody "needs" something from the church at this time. In addition, these overlapping needs are fertile terrain for a boundary violation, were Melody to seek pastoral care from Pastor Ellen in regard to her decision. It is just these sorts of conflicts of interest that working on a stakeholder map can uncover for the person in discernment. In the case of this example, Pastor Ellen will show up both on the stakeholder map of "discernment resources" and the map of "those with a stake in Melody's choice." It might be that Melody is feeling a bit ill at ease when she sees or talks with Pastor Ellen without knowing why. The stakeholder maps could help Melody understand her discomfort and make choices accordingly.

Mitch and Melody also have a number of resources upon which to draw. Melody could, where appropriate, turn to her educator parents for advice about education career paths. Her friend Amanda might provide an ongoing sounding board as an outsider with some insight into the family's situation. Mitch might have a mentor other than his supervisor who could guide him in finding more clarity about work expectations. All spiritual practices of discernment rely to some extent on the input of caring others. There is only so much any of us can or should work out on our own.

DATA COLLECTION AND ANALYSIS

Once Melody and Mitch have identified those who might help them with the decisions they need to make, they must figure out methodically whom to approach with which questions and what they are going to do with what they learn. By no means should they discount their gut feelings, but to make a gut-based decision about matters so complex and important would cut them off from other resources available to them.

DATA SOURCES	COLLECTION METHODS	ANALYSIS STRATEGY

Beyond caring others, Melody and Mitch can consider what sources of data are available to them: What can Melody learn through reading and talking with people about the work of a director of religious education? How will she gather that information, and what will she do with it when she has it? What is the state of the job market in Mitch's field, in their own region and elsewhere? Friedman writes that it is a mistake for leaders to value data more than they value decisiveness,[29] and yet it appears that Mitch and Melody made the opposite mistake with their first big decision—they went with their guts and what seemed expedient at the time. Ultimately, they chose a course of action that did not alleviate Mitch's work problems, nor did it answer Melody's vocational questions adequately. Now they must backtrack and try again, this time maximizing the information they have, not just about what is happening in the world around them but also about what is happening in their own hearts.

You may have noticed that, even when applying program planning and evaluation principles to an individual's life, I described the journeys of both Mitch and Melody. The decisions we all make in this complex world are intertwined with those of other people. When we make the choice to be part of families and churches and other relationships, we soon learn that it is rare for us to have a decision we can make in our own heads, alone.

Ministerial leaders make decisions alone at their peril. This past semester in my own life, for example, my associate director in the Andover Newton Field Education Program was on sabbatical. When she returned, I told her the job had been easier while she was away in that I did not need to discuss my decisions with anyone; I just made choices, and the chips fell. But I am so much better at my job when she is there! By having a wise conversation partner with whom to make sense of the context around us, the interventions we must bring into the setting, and the outcomes for which we hope, we all find greater clarity. Once my associate returned, I vowed that I would never again try to direct this program alone.

Faith Communities, Human Communities

At the beginning of this chapter, I described a day in December when I had to make a decision about how to divide my time between numerous conflicting commitments. To choose what obligations to give top priority, I talked with my husband and a couple of friends to get their insights. I considered how other people, most notably my daughter, would be affected by my choices. I even made a list of pros and cons. Ultimately, I chose to forego the alumni event for my college and wrote a note by e-mail to the planning committee, letting the group know that something had come up and that I could not attend. Instead, I volunteered at the church fair, my husband took our daughter to karate, and together we went as a family to our godchildren's birthday party. I learned later that attendance at the alumni event was dismal; I guess I was not the only one with competing commitments that day. Our daughter was thrilled by her new karate class. The table where I helped at the church fair sorely needed the extra set of hands. And our godchildren were aglow at their party. So I felt that I had made good choices and that we are lucky to have lives so full of joyful opportunities. Making choices is not always so easy.

The example of Melody and Mitch gives us insight into the way in which we *lead* our own lives and *lead* our own families. It is for this reason that leadership theory does have some bearing on individual and family life: we are all the CEOs of our choices and those of our families. In faith communities we often hear people reject corporate language as too bureaucratic and not religious. This illustration shows us that holy clarity helps us lead in all forms of human interaction, even interaction within our own minds, and that faith communities have this in common with business corporations, simply because both kinds of institutions involve *people*.

Throughout history, faith communities have come to mirror other sorts of institutions. But the key for understanding program planning and evaluation as a faith practice is to place it in the context of other forms of discernment from various movements in the Christian tradition. Methodical analysis of ourselves and our choices, in light of the work of the Spirit in our hearts, is part of a life of faith. Clarity does not always emerge spontaneously in our lives; we sometimes need to make it happen. And when we do, we can see more, know more, and feel more closely connected with our Creator.

Does God have a preordained will for our lives? Sometimes I think yes, and at other times I think that we are all just doing our best, with God's help, to cut a path toward a fuller and richer life. Sometimes, in the midst of our cutting (our actions), the branches part (God's action), and we see just where we need to go. In my experience, when I seek God's will, God meets me more than halfway by sending me signs that help answer my questions. When I make the effort to seek clarity, I believe that God rewards my efforts with strong signals, as well as a deep sense of satisfaction when clarity is attained. Perhaps that is the most compelling argument for the idea that I have presented in this book, that clarity is holy: when we find it, we feel good.

The logical question would then be: Why? Why does clarity feel good? And what is the nature of that goodness? In chapter 2, I wrote about four theological and biblical perspectives on clarity:

1. The inherent value of truth telling.
2. The intrinsic beauty of clarity.
3. The juxtaposition of blindness versus sight, both spiritual and physical.
4. The perfect clarity in the kingdom of God.

Connected to each of these four underpinnings of holy clarity we can identify a related human, emotional response. First, truth telling is a human act that I associate with trust, safety, and integrity, all of which feel good. The person living in the midst of a lie feels unsafe and ill at ease, as does a person living without clarity. Second, most rational people I know (and some irrational people) find a certain beauty in clear thinking, clear policies, and clearly defined leadership. They see elegance in institutions whose choices make sense, and in individuals who are clearly defined and self-possessed. Third, no one feels comfortable when "flying blind," trying to make decisions without understanding their surroundings. Although people who are blind sometimes demonstrate keen insights in other ways, blindness brings to mind negative feelings, such as confusion and disorientation. Finally, perfect clarity is something all of us associate with a certain ultimate truth, one that we cannot attain now but that we hope will come to pass in the next coming, or in the life beyond death.

These emotional corollaries to biblical and theological conceptions of holy clarity serve as drivers and motivators. These feelings help us continually to seek to clarify the lives we lead, the institutions we care about, and the faith communities we love. Just as the Jesuits teach us that God communicates with us through our emotions, the good feelings that come with holy clarity move us to seek it out wherever we can. Holy clarity is good, and in that goodness is a God who loves us and wants us to see the beauty God has in store for us in this life, and even in the next.

Notes

~

Preface

1. Marcia Festen and Marianne Philbin, *Level Best: How Small and Grassroots Nonprofits Can Tackle Evaluation and Talk Results* (San Francisco: Jossey-Bass, 2007), 51.

2. Festen and Philbin, *Level Best*, 4.

Chapter I

1. Lynn, former director of the religion division of Lilly Endowment Inc.'s Evaluation Project at Valparaiso University, provided this definition to evaluation coaches for the Lilly Endowment's Programs for the Theological Exploration of Vocation during a training session in 2006. I serve the religion division of Lilly Endowment Inc. as an evaluation coach, helping grantees build internal capacity for evaluation. It is important for readers to note, however, that although this work and training have been formative for my thinking, this book does not purport to speak on behalf of Lilly Endowment Inc. or represent that organization's philosophy of evaluation.

2. I use the terms "assessment" and "evaluation" interchangeably in this book.

3. Kathleen A. Cahalan, *Projects That Matter: Successful Planning and Evaluation for Religious Organizations* (Bethesda: Alban Institute, 2003), 9.

4. D. Susan Wisely, *Evaluation Notebook* (Indianapolis: Lilly Endowment, 1989), 5.

5. Festen and Philbin, *Level Best*, 66.

6. Craig Dykstra, "Evaluation as Collaborative Inquiry," *Initiatives in Religion* 2, no. 4 (fall 1993), *http://www.wabashcenter.edu/grants/article2.aspx?id=1011.*

7. Stanley N. Katz, "Taking the True Measure of a Liberal Education," *The Chronicle of Higher Education* (May 23, 2008): A32.

8. Wisely, *Evaluation Notebook*, 5.

9. Scott Cormode, *Making Spiritual Sense: Christian Leaders as Spiritual Interpreters* (Nashville: Abingdon, 2006), 66.

10. Robert D. Dale, *Leadership for a Changing Church: Charting the Shape of the River* (Nashville: Abingdon, 1998), 17.

11. The pastor was the Rev. Heather Kirk-Davidoff, preaching in the mid-1990s at Harvard Divinity School. Although I have no text from the service, I found this image powerful enough to remember it and use it to this day.

12. Jackson W. Carroll, *God's Potters: Pastoral Leadership and the Shaping of Congregations* (Grand Rapids: Eerdmans, 2006), 33.

13. Dale, *Leadership for a Changing Church*, 20.

14. Dale, *Leadership for a Changing Church*, 20.

15. Jill M. Hudson, *When Better Isn't Enough: Evaluation Tools for the 21st-Century Church* (Herndon, Va.: Alban Institute, 2004), 5.

16. I first heard this distinction in a class I taught at Andover Newton. The speaker was the Rev. Hope Luckie, a small-group leader for field education students at the time. I have since heard others use the image, and I have expanded upon it in my own interpretation of what it means to be a ministerial leader.

17. Hudson, *When Better Isn't Enough.*

18. Dale, *Leadership for a Changing Church*, 38.

19. John P. Kotter, *Leading Change* (Boston: Harvard Business School Press, 1996), 44.

20. Kotter, *Leading Change*, 90.

21. Cormode, *Making Spiritual Sense*, 25.

22. To read more about the current activities of the research project Pulpit & Pew, visit Duke University's website, *http://www.pulpitandpew.duke.edu* (accessed July 3, 2008).

23. L. Gregory Jones and Kevin R. Armstrong, *Resurrecting Excellence: Shaping Faithful Christian Ministry* (Grand Rapids: Eerdmans, 2006), 107.

24. Carroll, *God's Potters*, 56.

25. Carroll, *God's Potters*, 33.

26. Parker J. Palmer, *The Active Life: A Spirituality of Work, Creativity, and Caring* (San Francisco: Jossey-Bass, 1996).

27. Douglas J. Bixby, *Challenging the Church Monster: From Conflict to Community* (Eugene, Ore.: Wipf & Stock Publishers, 2007; original edition, Cleveland: Pilgrim Press, 2002), 27.

28. Bixby, *Challenging the Church Monster*, 36.

29. Cahalan, *Projects That Matter*, 31.

30. Festen and Philbin, *Level Best*, 2.

31. Nick Hornby, *High Fidelity* (New York: Riverhead Books, 1995), 315.

Chapter 2

1. I explored many of the themes and concepts from this section for the first time in a sermon at the Memorial Church, Harvard University, June 22, 2008.

2. Kathleen O'Connor, "Jeremiah," *The Oxford Bible Commentary*, John Barton and John Muddiman, eds. (Oxford, U.K.: Oxford University Press, 2001), 505.

3. Regina Coll, *Supervision of Ministry Students* (Collegeville, Minn.: Order of St. Benedict, 1992), 85–86.

4. Cormode, *Making Spiritual Sense*.

Chapter 3

1. Sharon Daloz Parks, *Leadership Can Be Taught: A Bold Approach for a Complex World* (Cambridge, Mass.: Harvard Business School Press, 2005), 9.

2. Evaluation Coach Training, May 2007, Indianapolis.

3. Hudson, *When Better Isn't Enough*, 102.

4. Hudson, *When Better Isn't Enough*, 99.

5. Festen and Philbin, *Level Best*, 8.

6. In *Level Best* Festen and Philbin write that this "overwhelmed and resentful" feeling comes from viewing evaluation as separate from your "real work" (p. 4). I take that concept in a different direction here.

7. Cahalan, *Projects That Matter*, 1.

8. Festen and Philbin, *Level Best*, 56.

9. Festen and Philbin write about process- and outcomes-evaluation, but I first learned the distinction from Susie Quern Pratt (see note 10, below).

10. "Signs of Success" exercise, evaluation coaching resource prepared by Susie Quern Pratt through the Evaluation Project, Valparaiso University.

11. Program Staff of the W. K. Kellogg Foundation, eds., *Logic Model Development Guide, http://www.wkkf.org/Pubs/Tools/Evaluation/Pub3669.pdfe* (accessed Sept. 11, 2008).

12. Cahalan, *Projects That Matter*, 36.

13. Cahalan, *Projects That Matter*, 58.

14. Cahalan, *Projects That Matter*, 58.

15. The fusing of these two models is an approach I borrow from Bill Millard at Indiana Wesleyan University, who uses this diagram in his own leadership and shared it with evaluation coaches in the Evaluation Project at Valparaiso University during a training session in 2006.

16. Festen and Philbin, *Level Best*, 15.

17. Cormode, *Making Spiritual Sense*, 88.

18. Cormode, *Making Spiritual Sense*, 49.

19. Daloz Parks, *Leadership Can Be Taught*, 9.

20. I thank my Andover Newton colleague, Maria Teresa Davila, for her help in creating realistic language (specifically, "parish council") for a Roman Catholic setting.

Chapter 4

1. Sarah B. Drummond, "Leading Change in Campus Religious Life: A Case Study on the Programs for the Theological Exploration of Vocation" (Ph.D. diss., University of Wisconsin–Milwaukee, 2005), 246.

2. Michael Fullan, *Leading in a Culture of Change* (San Francisco: Jossey-Bass, 2001), 44–45.

3. Kotter, *Leading Change*, 4.

4. Kotter, *Leading Change* 6.

5. Kotter, *Leading Change*, 7.

6. Kotter, *Leading Change*, 9.

7. Kotter, *Leading Change*, 10.

8. Kotter, *Leading Change*, 11.

9. Kotter, *Leading Change*, 12.

10. Kotter, *Leading Change*, 14.

11. Kotter, *Leading Change*, 21.

12. The university I served was the University of Wisconsin–Milwaukee, and the chancellor was Nancy Zimpher.

13. Sarah B. Drummond, "Learning, Leadership, and Rapid Change," *Journal of Religious Leadership* 6, no. 1 (spring 2007): 103–21.

14. Drummond, "Leading Change in Campus Religious Life," 246.

15. Bixby, *Challenging the Church Monster*, 51.

16. Kotter, *Leading Change*, 64.

17. The visitors to my class (Ministerial Leadership in Program Planning and Evaluation, Andover Newton Theological School, spring 2008) were the Revs. J. Mary Luti and Daniel Smith from First Church in Cambridge, Mass., United Church of Christ.

18. See notes 13 and 14, where I cite references in which I offered similar arguments.

19. Kotter, *Leading Change*, 125.

20. This resource is adapted from the Evaluation Project at Valparaiso University.

21. Cahalan, *Projects That Matter*, 87.

22. Jones and Armstrong, *Resurrecting Excellence*, 4.

23. Cahalan, *Projects That Matter*, 47.

Chapter 5

1. Dorothy Bass, ed., *Practicing Our Faith: A Way of Life for a Searching People* (San Francisco: Jossey Bass, 1997).

2. Dorothy Bass and Craig Dykstra, "Times of Yearning, Practices of Faith," in *Practicing Our Faith*, 6.

3. Bass and Dykstra, "Times of Yearning," 6–8.

4. Bass and Dykstra, "Times of Yearning," 2.

5. Bass and Dykstra, *Practicing Our Faith*, 195.

6. Since they visited my course, Mary Luti has joined the faculty at the seminary where I teach, and her colleague Dan Smith has been called as the church's new senior pastor.

7. Brochure "God's Vision For Us: A Way of Hospitality," produced by First Church in Cambridge, Congregational, United Church of Christ.

8. "God's Vision for Us."

9. Final Grant Report to the Valparaiso Project: "Heritage, Hospitality and Wholeness: Responding to God's Vision for Us," First Church in Cambridge, Congregational, United Church of Christ.

10. Brochure "Small Groups," produced by First Church in Cambridge, Congregational, United Church of Christ.

11. Final Grant Report, FCC, 5–6.

12. Final Grant Report, FCC, 6.

13. Final Grant Report, FCC, 7.

14. Cahalan, *Projects That Matter*, 9.

15. Nick Carter, Syllabus, Strategic Planning, Andover Newton Theological School, January term 2009.

16. Laurence A. Parks Daloz, Cheryl H. Keen, James P. Keen, and Sharon Daloz Parks, *Common Fire: Leading Lives of Commitment in a Complex World* (Boston: Beacon Press, 1996).

Chapter 6

1. Edwin H. Friedman. *A Failure of Nerve: Leadership in the Age of the Quick Fix* (New York: Church Publishing, Inc., 1999, 2007).

2. Friedman, *A Failure of Nerve*, 14.

3. Friedman, *A Failure of Nerve*, 13, 49.

4. Friedman, *A Failure of Nerve*, 8.

5. Friedman, *A Failure of Nerve*, 32.

6. Friedman, *A Failure of Nerve*, 31.

7. Marie M. Fortune, Frances E. Wood, Elizabeth A. Stellas, Rebecca Voelkel, Deborah Woolley Lindsay, and Judith K. Applegate, *Clergy Misconduct: Sexual Abuse in the Ministerial Relationship.* (Seattle: FaithTrust Institute, 1992, 1997), 37.

8. Fortune et al., *Clergy Misconduct*.

9. Fortune et al., *Clergy Misconduct*.

10. Frank Rogers, Jr., "Discernment," in Dorothy C. Bass, ed., *Practicing Our Faith: A Way of Life for a Searching People* (San Francisco: Jossey-Bass, 1997), 107.

11. Rogers, "Discernment," 107.

12. Rogers, "Discernment," 107.

13. Rogers, "Discernment," 108.

14. Rogers, "Discernment," 109.

15. Parker Palmer. *Let Your Life Speak: Listening for the Voice of Vocation* (San Francisco: Jossey Bass, 2000), 44.

16. Rogers, "Discernment," 107.

17. Rogers, "Discernment," 111.

18. Friedman, *A Failure of Nerve*, 203.

19. Friedman, *A Failure of Nerve*, 197.

20. Friedman, *A Failure of Nerve*, 196.

21. Friedman, *A Failure of Nerve*, 198–199.

22. Friedman, *A Failure of Nerve*, 197.

23. Friedman, *A Failure of Nerve*, 14.

24. Friedman, *A Failure of Nerve*, 201.

25. Friedman, *A Failure of Nerve*, 53–54.

26. Rogers, "Discernment," 107.
27. Friedman, *A Failure of Nerve*, 96.
28. Friedman, *A Failure of Nerve*, 201.
29. Friedman, *A Failure of Nerve*, 49.